SEEK HER OUT

A Textual Approach to the
Study of Women and Judaism

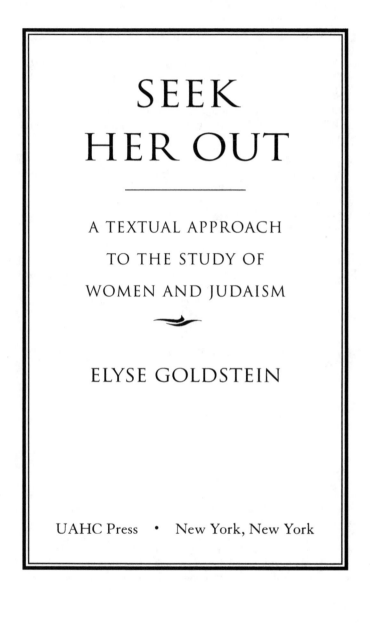

SEEK
HER OUT

A TEXTUAL APPROACH
TO THE STUDY OF
WOMEN AND JUDAISM

ELYSE GOLDSTEIN

UAHC Press   •   New York, New York

The author gratefully acknowledges the following for granting permission to reprint previously published material:

CENTRAL CONFERENCE OF AMERICAN RABBIS: Excerpt from *Gates of Repentance,* © 1978, is copyright by Central Conference of American Rabbis and is reproduced by permission; excerpts from *CCAR Journal: A Reform Jewish Quarterly* 44 (summer 1997) are copyright by Central Conference of American Rabbis and are reproduced by permission.

KTAV PUBLISHING HOUSE, INC.: Excerpts from *A Jewish Mourner's Handbook,* © 1991, by Ron H. Isaacs and Kerry M. Olitzky. Reprinted by permission of KTAV Publishing House.

REFORM JUDAISM: Quotes by Andy Curry and Rabbi Elyse Goldstein from "Letters to the Editor" in *Reform Judaism* 26 (summer 1998) are excerpted with permission of *Reform Judaism* magazine, published by the Union of American Hebrew Congregations; excerpt from "Jewish Macho" by Jeffrey K. Salkin in *Reform Judaism* 26 (summer 1998) is excerpted with permission of *Reform Judaism* magazine, published by the Union of American Hebrew Congregations, and with permission of Rabbi Jeffrey Salkin.

ELIZABETH TIKVAH SARAH: "Meditation for Tefillin" by Rabbi Elizabeth Tikvah Sarah. Copyright © Elizabeth Tikvah Sarah. Previously appeared in *Taking Up the Timbrel* edited by Sylvia Rothschild and Sybil Sheridan (London, England: SCM Press, 2000) and *The Dybbuk of Delight: An Anthology of Jewish Women's Poetry* edited by Sylvia Paskin and Sonja Lyndon (Nottingham, England: Five Leaves Publications, 1995). Reprinted by permission of Rabbi Elizabeth Tikvah Sarah.

SIMON & SCHUSTER: Excerpts reprinted with the permission of Simon & Schuster from *The New Jewish Wedding* by Anita Diamant. Copyright © 1985 by Anita Diamant.

Library of Congress Cataloging-in-Publication Data

Goldstein, Elyse.
    Seek her out : a textual approach to the study of women and Judaism
    / Elyse Goldstein.
        p. cm.
    Includes bibliographical references.
    Contents: Women and Torah—Women and halachah—Women and
    ritual—Women and theology—Women and leadership.
    ISBN 0-8074-0817-4 (pbk. : alk. paper)
    1. Women in Judaism. 2. Women in the Bible. 3. Women—Legal
    status, laws, etc. (Jewish law) 4. Jewish women—Religious life.
    5. Femininity of God. 6. Feminism—Religious aspects—Judaism. I. Title.

BM729.W6G66 2003
296'.082—dc21   2003056364

Contents

Acknowledgments

Several times over the past years Rabbi Hara Person of the UAHC Press has asked me, encouraged me, taken me out to fancy dinners in order to convince me, and downright cajoled me into writing a textbook on women and Judaism. It is due to my great respect for her, for the UAHC, and for the people I hope to be teaching through this book that she finally succeeded! I owe a special thank you to her for her clear vision of why this book is so important.

I have taught the issues contained in this book for many years to a wide variety of groups, and it is to my students that I owe a debt of gratitude for opening their hearts and minds to my teachings: to my first congregants at Holy Blossom temple in Toronto (whom I convinced in 1983 to form a "feminist Torah study group"), then to my congregants at Temple Beth David in Canton, Massachusetts (and to the stalwart and steady group of men who always attended my "women and Judaism" classes there), and finally to the numerous groups of adults who have taken courses at Kolel: The Adult Centre for Liberal Jewish Learning in Toronto, where I returned to serve. My adult students set the context for this book, and it was their striving with the complex and often emotional issues around the ever-changing roles of women in their synagogues, organizations, and homes that led to its being written. Thank you to my husband, Baruch, and three sons, Noam, Carmi, and Micah, for their endless patience as I type away into the night and for their embracing love and passion for Judaism, which makes them the perfect sounding board for many of my ideas.

I would also like to thank all those at the UAHC Press who took good care of this book, including Ken Gesser, Joel Eglash, Liane Broido, Debra Hirsch Corman, and Annie Belford.

Introduction

There is no doubt that the proliferation of women's study groups, Rosh Chodesh groups, and resources for those exploring the issues of gender and Judaism attests to the explosion not only of interest in the subject, but to the extent of seriousness in pursuing it. Twenty years ago, "women and Judaism" courses were a fad, a nod to the populist culture, and an appeasement to "uppity" Sisterhood ladies questioning their traditional role in the synagogue. Today, there is hardly a congregation, school, youth group, or women's organization without some scholarly or rabbinic investigation of this topic in its regular curriculum.

Now that we have "women and Judaism" courses, we can see that we have been studying "men and Judaism" all along, mistakenly believing we had been learning "just Judaism." We have assumed that what we received was a neutral form of Judaism. There is no such thing as "neutral" or "just Judaism," because by hearing the same stories retold by women, by being at the same events led by women, by simply sitting in the pews and looking up to see women in front of us, we have grown to understand that the Judaism we inherited was filtered through men and the male experience.

In the early years of the new studies in "women and Judaism," the questions centered around equality and equal access, and the early cry of "Jewish women's lib" was for the same opportunities, responsibilities, and access to resources as men. The issue seemed simple enough: the biological differences between men and women should not translate themselves into social barriers. Although men and women differ biologically, they are essentially the same. Thus both proponents *and* opponents of early "women's lib" defined equality as sameness.

Today's "women and Judaism" has entered a second phase. We no longer believe that to be equal to men religiously and spiritually we have to be like men. Indeed, the question has come from its original roots in equal access. We now ask if it is possible to *specialize* as women while we *equalize* as women. We want to know if there is a unique "woman's way" of seeing and hearing the text, of practicing the traditions, of living the rituals, that might be different from what we have received. We are no longer so completely convinced that women and men are essentially the same. Do we see and experience the world differently than men do because we are women? Does being female so influence our perceptions of ourselves that it also colors the way we perceive the rest of life and everything around us? If so, how does gender affect our religious life?

Do not assume that "women and Judaism" is no longer an issue, is over and done with, in the egalitarian movements. Though the Reform Movement began ordaining women in the 1970s, with the Reconstructionist and Conservative Movements following suit, the "women and Judaism" question has not gone away with the advent of equal access. For egalitarianism does not insist upon women's voices *as women* being heard, women's perspectives *as women* being sought, women's experiences *as women* being recorded. It assumes a spiritual equality, a halachic equality, even a ritual equality, but it has not yet dealt with the question of *difference*.

There are three areas into which the questions seem to fall. The first is in the area of Torah. How does the Torah deal with women? Are they central characters, marginal characters, or both? And what does this question assume about the way we study Torah? In the first part of this book, we will study women in the Torah in a generic sense. Though we will not look at specific women, we will ask how the portrayal of women affects our reading of women's place in biblical Judaism. We will study the question of power and powerlessness, of women as property or persons, and we will finish by looking at *Eishet Chayil,* "A Woman of Valor," as a prime example of the overarching ambivalence of the Torah about the "one, right role" of women.

The second is the arena of ritual. The questions of traditional halachah fall into this area, in which the questions arise as to whether women can or cannot, should or should not perform certain rituals. We will study some of those permissions and prohibitions, with an eye to the more general question of the role of women in the synagogue. We will also look at "new" women's rituals and ask if they solve some of the traditional challenges while also creating new ones. In this second part, we will also delve into the biblical treatment of menstruation. Is there something positive in the Torah's menstrual taboos that we can modernize, spiritualize, and see in a new light?

And the third area of this book is theology. What shall we use for God language, and why? Why does the way in which we talk about God matter so much? He, She, It, *Shechinah,* God, Goddess: what role should history and tradition play in the evolving discussion of how we speak about the Divine?

This book is written from a liberal perspective, and thus it does, in a sense, "pitch" that position. But the book is meant to be used both in a class setting and as a self-directed textbook, and readers are encouraged to come to their own conclusions and answer the questions in their own ways.

Since all translation from one language into another has within it an element of interpretation, it is hard to find any one translation that is truest to the original Hebrew. For the sections of Torah in this book, I have relied heavily upon the Jewish Publication Society translation found within *The Torah: A Modern Commentary,* edited by Rabbi Gunther Plaut, adding to it or expressing my own understanding of a nuance in the verse. Thus the Torah sections quoted within are a combination of my own translation and the scholarship of others. All of the traditional rabbinic texts are my own translations.

A word about "self-direction." We know, from both the secular literature and more recent Jewish exploration into the professional world of adult education, that the one thing that differentiates adult learners from children is their ability to direct their own learning, its outcomes, and its procedures. That is why this is intended to work as a *self-directed adult textbook*. Readers are encouraged all along the way to follow the template of introduction, text study, and questions, but if a different order appeals to you, by all means try it. The questions at the end of each section are meant to stimulate discussion and critical thinking. Add your own, change the questions to fit your group or class, and rearrange the questions as you see fit. You will notice there is no section for "answers." There is no key at the end to the "right" solutions, for the discussions themselves should prove how multifaceted the responses can be. Group leaders, teachers, or rabbis can use these questions as jumping-off points for longer and deeper studies of the issues, or self-directed groups can see the questions as discussion starters. Feel free to use the texts and questions even as homework or projects for the participants.

In the end, I hope you will find that the adage of Ben Bag Bag in *Pirkei Avot* rings true for you: turn it, turn it, for everything is in it. There is no area in Jewish thinking that has not been affected by the revolution in consciousness around gender issues. Each of the areas I present here is a small mirror of what is being asked in synagogues, study groups, adult education centers, and retreats across the world. May you take your place in this ongoing exploration and be enriched and enlightened from your study. *Zil g'mor:* go and learn.

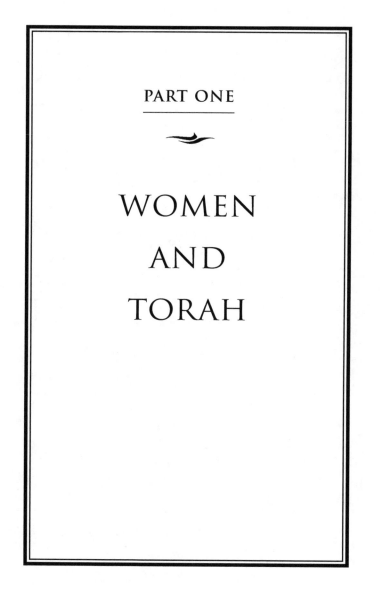

PART ONE

WOMEN

AND

TORAH

1

Feminist Analysis and Torah Study

What is a "feminist analysis" of Torah? Such an analysis would begin with the notion that because of their life experiences, and from the simple fact of being women all their lives in a still male-dominated society, women see the text differently than do men, ask different questions, and bring different answers. A feminist analysis would look at all the stories of the Torah as enmeshed within a patriarchal interpretation and culture, in which it is not clear whether women are or are not classified as "real" members of the tribe. It assumes that the Torah sees women as part of the enterprise, but not as its center. Feminist analysis might deconstruct in order to reconstruct. It would ask of the Torah, "How ennobling is this story for women? How are this character's actions reflective of a respect for women?"

Unfortunately, there is still a lack of female traditional Torah interpretations; there is, as of now, no recently unearthed manuscript attributed to Rashi's daughter. Commentary was the realm of the learned man and was closed to women for many centuries. But in this generation we finally do have brilliant feminist scholars who have taken up serious biblical commentary. We also have homiletics—the traditional methodology used for interpreting the text through story, parable, sermon, discourse, and the like—that are feminist. We have fantasies and tales that lend a human face—indeed a female one—to the sacred text.

A variety of ways now exist of seeing the Torah through a feminist lens. The more methodical feminist works can be grouped into three categories: rejectionist, inventive, and revisionist.

The *rejectionist* school repudiates the Torah outright. The Torah, rejectionists say, cannot be salvaged. It offers no hope for women. In fact, it systematically takes hope from women. It presents a picture of woman and womanhood that is completely "other." They say, "Equality for women never was, it never will be. Trying to find it, or inventing it, is a deception." Such women have either left organized religion; remained only culturally connected to their religion; chosen goddess, neo-pagan, and witch religions; or chosen religious scholarship wholly critical of the Torah.

The *inventive* writers are midrashists. They reappropriate the rabbinic use of parable, story, and metaphor, creating explications and interpretations called *midrash* in Hebrew. They look deeply into the biblical texts and, failing to find women's voices or women's experience, *invent* it. Like the classical midrashists, they may wander far from the original at times. Like the traditional midrashists, they add characters, provide dialogue, change scenes, and suggest alternative readings. Reading Sarah into the *Akeidah,* supplying Rebekah's feelings at the well, naming Lot's wife—all of these are inventive and fill in the details of women's lives, women's thoughts, hopes, and dreams.

The third group, the *revisionists,* believe that with all its problems, the Torah is still, at its core, a powerful and even liberating document; that within the Torah there is evidence of women valued for their personhood, women as spiritual individuals and women as central players in Jewish history; that the Torah is not first and foremost about women as secondary, oppressed sub-citizens. There may even be instances we can uncover of women fighting the system and rebelling against their own oppression. Such a reading would say, "It's there—we just have to find it! It was. It existed!" Revisionists recognize patriarchy in the Torah but invite us to read the Torah with nonpatriarchal eyes. They reject the layers of later sexism and male commentary that have covered over and, in some ways, negated the original text. Most modern feminist scholars would probably classify themselves as revisionists.

Feminist methodologies include:

1. A critique of the text from within its social context as that context applies to women both in the biblical period and now.
2. A critique of the traditional ways of "unpacking" the text that rarely "unpacked" it for women.
3. An analysis of the assumptions we bring to the text, based on a history of our own personal biases we have inherited from a patriarchal Judaism.
4. Messages of change within a traditional reverence for an unchanging text, that is, the paradox of being agents of change who still maintain tradition.
5. A correction of the so-called "neutral" commentaries that came before. This calls into question the marginality of feminist discussion and offers the opportunity to go back and examine the "neutrality" of what we have learned before.
6. Questions: Where are women in the story? Are they visible, and if not, why not? Does this story teach us anything about the "character" of woman? Or does it teach us about the biases of the male lens through which the story is viewed?

In addition to these three approaches, there is also a school of *apologetics,* which claims that oppression simply does not occur in the Torah. Like its name, such scholars apologize for seeming inequities in the text by claiming that in actuality there are no cases of women treated as second-class citizens and no injustices to women in the halachic-legal system posited by the Torah. These apologists respond with justifications and rationales to every critique and claim that if we just understood the Torah better, we would clearly see how wonderfully women are portrayed and how our original concerns are misbegotten. There may be some instances where women "appear" to be aggrieved or "perhaps" are depicted in a negative light, but these few instances can be easily fixed by traditional commentators. *Apologists generally claim that the problem lies not in the text but in the reader.* They believe the text is misunderstood by the reader when it "appears" unjust or sexist. The text is held to be essentially enlightened for women, with isolated cracks that can be mended through exegesis and the beauty of a traditional life. These commentaries are not systematic critiques nor revisions nor feminist reexaminations. Although some appropriate the term "feminist," they are essentially interested in converting the complainer to their point of view: that there really is nothing about which to complain.

The layers of Torah are many, rich, and complex. One must search and search again to uncover all its many meanings, some obvious, some hidden, some obtuse, some clear. Feminist analysis adds yet another layer that deepens the study while challenging the student.

THE TEXTS

1. *Rejectionist:* Naomi Goldenberg, *Changing of the Gods* (Boston: Beacon Press, 1979), 10, 13, 22:

   > Although I admire the efforts of the reformers, I see them engaged in a hopeless effort. . . . Many feminists recommend ignoring parts of the Torah, but still claim the book as a whole is God-given. It is hard to deny that an eventual consequence of criticizing the correctness of any sacred text or tradition is to question why that text or tradition should be considered a divine authority at all. . . . In order to develop a theology of women's liberation, feminists have to leave . . . the Bible behind them.

2. *Inventive:* Rachel Adler, *Engendering Judaism* (Philadelphia, Jewish Publication Society, 1998), 38:

   > One crucial contribution will be the methodologies feminists have developed for understanding and using narrative. . . . As a method of vision, feminist narratives draw upon fantasies and desires, prophecies and prayers to imagine possible worlds in which both women and men could flourish. As a tool of critique, narrative can expose within abstract theories assumptions about the nature and experience of being human, what people know, how they love, what they want, and what they fear.

3. *Revisionist:* Mary Ann Tolbert, "Defining the Problem: The Bible and Feminist Hermeneutics," *Semeia* 28 (1983), 122:

   > It is a "conscious effort to retrieve texts overlooked or distorted by patriarchal hermeneutics . . . (it) focuses its attention on texts involving women characters and explores their functions without the patriarchal presumption of marginality. . . . To find within the writings of a culture so thoroughly patriarchal any counter-cultural material witnesses to the theological vitality and the importance of that remnant."

THE QUESTIONS

1. Read the Goldenberg quote. Where does it leave feminists who wish to take the Bible seriously but also wish to reject its sexism? Are we just playing loose and fast with a truly sexist text? If we totally reject the Torah as a divine text, what is it to us?

2. Tolbert believes we are able to find countercultural voices within the biblical text itself by being inventive. Read the following with that in mind:

> ### The Women of the Exodus Story
>
> The "boys" of the Exodus story follow the rules with the notable exception of the Golden Calf. The "girls" work secretly against the rules, in favor of the value of human relationships. The "boys" accept the rules at Sinai and get a reward: the priesthood, the land, tribal heads. But it is the "girls" who keep the system running through their empathy and compassion. . . .
>
> Pharaoh commands that the boys are to be killed, the girls left alive. In a male-centered polygamous society, girls are sexually useful as future wives and concubines. Boys as future enemy soldiers pose a clearer threat. As sons of an enslaved population, they wait to fill their roles as future rebels. Yet Pharaoh didn't understand that girls and women bonding together against him might provide a different, unexpected rebellion.[1]

   a) How were the women of the Exodus story an example of a "different, unexpected rebellion"? Read the following texts on Shiphrah and Puah, and on Yocheved and Miriam.

   (1) Shiphrah and Puah (Exodus 1:5–17):

> The king of Egypt spoke to the Hebrew midwives, one of whom was named Shiphrah and one of whom was named Puah, saying: "When you deliver the Hebrew women, look at the birthing-stool. If it is a boy, kill him; if it is a girl, let her live." The midwives feared God and did not do as the king of Egypt had said; they let the boys live!

(2) Yocheved and Miriam (Exodus 2:2–4):

> The woman conceived and bore a son, and when she saw he was a good [or: docile?] child, she hid him for three months. When she could hide him no longer, she got a wicker basket and caulked it with bitumen and pitch. She placed the child into it and put it among the reeds on the bank of the Nile. And his sister stationed herself at a distance to see what would happen to him.

b) Moses was adopted by Pharaoh's daughter and brought back to his mother for nursing. Read the following text (Exodus 2:5–9). How is this a rebellion of sorts?

> The daughter of Pharaoh came down to bathe in the Nile, while her maidens walked along the Nile. She saw the basket in the reeds and sent her servant to fetch it. When she opened it, she saw it was a child; indeed, it was a boy crying. She took pity on it and said, "This must be a Hebrew child." Then his sister said to Pharaoh's daughter, "Shall I go and acquire for you a wet-nurse from the Hebrews and she will nurse the child for you?" And Pharaoh's daughter answered, "Yes." So the girl went and called the child's mother. And Pharaoh's daughter said to her, "Take this child and nurse it for me, and I shall pay your wages."

Was Pharaoh's daughter somehow "involved" more than the text lets on? Can you imagine an "underground railroad" at work here?

c) How did the women of the Exodus story work together? Can you "invent" a midrash that places them all in the same place at the same time? What would they be doing?

3. Read the two stories of the creation of woman:
   a) Genesis 1:26–29:

> And God said, Let us make *adam* in our image, in our likeness. They shall rule the fish of the sea, the birds of the sky, the cattle, the whole earth, and all the creeping things that creep on earth. And God created the *adam* in God's image, in the image of God was it created; male and female God created them. And God blessed them and said to them, "Be fruitful and multiply. . . ."

b) Genesis 2:18–25:

> *Adonai* God said, "It is not good for the *adam* [or: the man] to be alone; I will make a fitting helper for him/it [or: a helper in opposition to him/it]." And *Adonai* God formed out of the earth all the wild beasts and all the birds of the sky, and brought them to the *adam* to see what it would call them. Whatever the *adam* called each living creature, that would be its name. And the *adam* gave names to all the cattle and the birds of the sky and to all the wild beasts; but for *adam* no fitting helper was found. So *Adonai* God cast a deep sleep upon the *adam,* and while he slept, God took one of his sides [or: ribs] and closed up the flesh at that spot. And *Adonai* God fashioned the side that He had taken from the *adam* into a woman, and He brought her to the *adam.* Then the *adam* said, "This one, this time, is bone of my bones and flesh of my flesh. She shall be called woman, for from man was she taken."

Analyze these two accounts using rejectionist, inventive, and revisionist schools of thought. How would each school view the texts, and how would each deal with the apparent "contradiction" in these two accounts? What might apologists say?

4. Are there limits to feminist analysis? How do we know when we have gone "too far"? Is there a "too far" and based on what criteria?

2

~

"Womanhood" in the *Tanach*:
Persons or Property?

THE ISSUES

When we ask what the role of women in the Torah is, there are no easy or clear answers. First, it depends on the reason for the question. For some, the question is political: one may wish to prove or disprove a certain theory that women are, for example, merely chattel in the Torah or, conversely, that women are exalted and important persons in their own right. So the answers, and the proof texts to support those answers, are usually carefully chosen to lend support to a preconceived notion.

Second, it depends on what you mean by role. Ancient societies were often strictly divided on hierarchical and class lines: man or woman, child or adult, slave or free, poor or rich, with or without land, were all important legal categories. By role, do we mean rights? Responsibilities? Privileges? Or all of those?

And third, it depends on how objective we can be when we judge past societies by the standards of today. When we ask how much power biblical women had, we must first examine what women's power meant during biblical times. We should not assume that our foremothers would have exercised power in the same way we do today. Did our female ancestors recognize the existing power structure as oppressive to them? Did they see themselves as preservers of that system or as victims of it? As "the power behind the throne" (as manipulators of men), did women ever hold true power? Or was this methodology of gaining control the only one open and available to our foremothers in the Torah?

On one level, women in biblical days exercised power in the ways we would stereotype as "women's ways" but that we reject today. They manipulated, pleaded, and deceived. Yet on another level, they decided, organized, and resisted, which must have been difficult given the cultural expectations of proper female behavior in their day. *Our foremothers were powerful in their own context, though not necessarily in ours.* So while our foremothers lived within and were controlled by the structures of their day, and this control affected their ability ultimately to transform those structures, they also achieved success in shaping Jewish history, tribal destiny, and their own small worlds.

In the Torah, women are complex subjects and objects. They are not subjugated and denied their rights, but they are not prominent, powerful center-stage actors. The women of the Torah weave in and out of the frames of both power and powerlessness. They act both as independent agents and as subjects. They work within the patriarchal structure to change it for their own benefit, as in the story of the daughters of Zelophehad, but they do not challenge the underlying structure of inequality for all women. They are fully human: they are curious, desirous, jealous, cooperative, and co-opted. Sometimes they act like "stereotypical" women, and sometimes they do not.

Interestingly, many male biblical characters work alone or, when in relationship, are in conflict with one another. Abraham barely speaks to his son Isaac as they walk up the mountain in an episode of near-sacrifice. Cain and Abel, Jacob and Esau are adversaries. Isaac and Ishmael, the two sons of Abraham, were once close, but end up separated. In contrast, we observe the cooperative efforts of sisters Leah and Rachel when it is time to leave Laban's house, the daughters of Zelophehad who organize in the desert and claim an inheritance of their father's land, and the women of the Exodus story who unite against Pharaoh.

So how do we define an individual's real power? Is it use of one's ability to manipulate, convince, or coerce? Is it charisma? Is it knowledge? Is it leadership skills? Or is it the ability to bond people together, form communities, and cooperate? The lens through which we have seen the women of the Torah has been a male one, determined by a rabbinic tradition that has valued and extensively written about their femininity. In that context, their strength—seen as "stereotypically female"—has been devalued.

In truth, woman in the Torah is both person and property. Woman is both powerful and powerless. That may be an unsatisfying answer for those who had wanted a black or white answer. But as discussed earlier, this ambiguity is part of the rich complexity of Torah.

THE TEXTS

The underlying tension in the Torah is between women as "persons" and women as "property." In a polygamous society, women tend to be valued objects, like cattle or jewels—the more you have, the richer you appear to be. Women can be traded like commodities, given away or sold, yet they are commanded to keep all the laws of the Sabbath and Festivals, and accorded respect and honor as part of the family.

Woman as Property

1. Exodus 20:14 lists women among the things a man "has":

    "You shall not covet your neighbor's house, you shall not covet your neighbor's wife, nor his manservant, nor his maidservant, nor his ox, nor his ass, nor anything that is your neighbor's."

2. According to Deuteronomy 22:13–21, a husband may publicly challenge his wife's virginity (and she has to stay married to him if he is proved wrong by her father, who brings forth undefined "signs of her virginity"):

    If any man takes a wife, and goes in to her, and hates her, and gives accusing speeches against her, and brings an evil name upon her, and says, "I took this woman, and when I came to her, I did not find in her the signs of virginity," then shall the father of the girl, and her mother, take and bring forth the signs of the girl's virginity to the elders of the city in the gate. And the girl's father shall say to the elders, "I gave my daughter to this man to wife, and he hates her; and, behold, he has given accusing speeches against her, saying, 'I found not your daughter a virgin'; and yet these are the signs of my daughter's virginity." And they shall spread the cloth before the elders of the city. And the elders of that city shall take that man and chastise him; and they shall fine him a hundred shekels of silver, and give them to the father of the girl, because he has brought up an evil name upon a virgin of Israel; and she shall be his wife; he may not put her away all his days. But if this thing is true, and the signs of virginity are not found for the girl, then they shall bring out the girl to the door of her father's house, and the men of her city shall stone her with stones that she die; because she has perpetrated wantonness in Israel, to play the harlot in her father's house; so shall you put evil away from among you.

3. Although women are equally able as men to make vows, a father can cancel his daughter's vows or a husband can cancel his wife's vows (Numbers 30:4–14):

> If a woman also vows a vow to *Adonai* and binds herself by a bond, being in her father's house in her youth, and her father hears her vow and her bond with which she has bound her soul and her father shall hold his peace at her, then all her vows shall stand, and every bond with which she has bound her soul shall stand. But if her father disallows her in the day that he hears, not one of her vows or of her bonds with which she has bound her soul shall stand; and *Adonai* shall forgive her, because her father disallowed her. And if she had a husband when she vowed or uttered anything out of her lips with which she bound her soul, and her husband heard it and held his peace at her in the day that he heard it, then her vows shall stand, and her bonds with which she bound her soul shall stand. But if her husband disallowed her on the day that he heard it, then he shall make her vow which she vowed and that which she uttered with her lips with which she bound her soul of no effect; and *Adonai* shall forgive her. But every vow of a widow and of her who is divorced, with which they have bound their souls, shall stand against her. And if she vowed in her husband's house or bound her soul by a bond with an oath, and her husband heard it, and held his peace at her, and disallowed her not, then all her vows shall stand, and every bond with which she bound her soul shall stand. But if her husband has utterly made them void on the day he heard them, then whatever proceeded out of her lips concerning her vows or concerning the bond of her soul shall not stand; her husband has made them void, and *Adonai* shall forgive her. Every vow, and every binding oath to afflict the soul, her husband may establish it, or her husband may make it void.

4. A husband can publicly humiliate his wife if he even suspects her of adultery or a "spirit of jealousy" comes over him (Numbers 5:12–31):

> Speak to the people of Israel, and say to them: If any man's wife goes astray and commits a trespass against him, and a man lies with

her carnally, and it is hidden from the eyes of her husband, and this is kept undetected, and she is defiled, and there is no witness against her, since she was not caught in the act; and the spirit of jealousy comes upon him, and he is jealous of his wife, and she is defiled; or if the spirit of jealousy comes upon him, and he is jealous of his wife, and she is not defiled; then shall the man bring his wife to the priest, and he shall bring her offering for her, the tenth part of an ephah of barley meal; he shall pour no oil upon it, nor put frankincense on it; for it is an offering of jealousy, an offering of memorial, bringing iniquity to remembrance. And the priest shall bring her near, and set her before *Adonai;* and the priest shall take holy water in an earthen utensil; and of the dust that is in the floor of the Tabernacle the priest shall take and put it into the water; and the priest shall set the woman before *Adonai,* and loosen the hair of the woman's head, and put the offering of memorial in her hands, which is the meal offering of jealousy; and the priest shall have in his hand the bitter water that causes the curse. And the priest shall charge her by an oath, and say to the woman, "If no man has lain with you, and if you have not gone astray to uncleanness with another instead of your husband, be you free from this bitter water that causes the curse; but if you have gone astray with another instead of your husband, and if you are defiled, and some man has lain with you other than your husband"; then the priest shall charge the woman with an oath of cursing, and the priest shall say to the woman, "*Adonai* make you a curse and an oath among your people, when *Adonai* makes your thigh fall away, and your belly swell. And this water that causes the curse shall go into your bowels, to make your belly swell, and your thigh to fall away." And the woman shall say, "Amen, amen." And the priest shall write these curses in a book, and he shall blot them out with the bitter water; and he shall cause the woman to drink the bitter water that causes the curse; and the water that causes the curse shall enter into her and become bitter. Then the priest shall take the meal offering of jealousy from the woman's hand, and shall wave the offering before *Adonai,* and offer it upon the altar; and the priest shall take a handful of the offering, its memorial, and burn it upon the altar, and afterward shall cause the woman to drink the water. And when he has made her drink the water, then it shall come to pass, that, if she is defiled and has trespassed against her husband, the water that causes the curse shall enter into her, and become bitter, and her belly shall swell, and her thigh shall fall; and the woman shall be a curse among her people. And if the woman is not defiled, but is clean; then she shall be free and shall conceive seed. This is the Torah of jealousies, when a wife goes astray with another instead of her husband, and is defiled; or when the spirit of jealousy comes upon him, and he is jealous over his wife, and shall set the woman before *Adonai,* and the priest shall execute upon her all this Torah. Then shall the man be guiltless from iniquity, and this woman shall bear her iniquity.

Woman as Person

1. Respect for a mother, no less than for a father, is one of the Ten Commandments (Exodus 20:12):

   Honor your father and your mother, that your days may be long upon the land that *Adonai* your God gives you.

2. Five women together, the daughters of Zelophehad, success-fully change the inheritance laws to include daughters (Numbers 27:1–8):

   Then came the daughters of Zelophehad, the son of Hepher, the son of Gilead, the son of Machir, the son of Manasseh, of the families of Manasseh the son of Joseph; and these are the names of his daughters: Mahlah, Noah, and Hoglah, and Milcah, and Tirzah. And they stood before Moses, and before Eleazar the priest, and before the princes and all the congregation, by the door of the Tent of Meeting, saying, "Our father died in the wilderness, and he was not in the company of those who gathered themselves together against *Adonai* in the company of Korah; but died in his own sin, and had no sons. Why should the name of our father be taken away from among his family, because he had no sons? Give to us therefore a possession among the brothers of our father." And Moses brought their cause before *Adonai.* And *Adonai* spoke to Moses, saying, "The daughters of Zelophehad speak right; you shall surely give them a possession of an inheritance among their father's brothers; and you shall cause the inheritance of their father to pass to them. And you shall speak to the people of Israel, saying, 'If a man dies, and has no son, then you shall cause his inheritance to pass to his daughter.'"

3. No father can force his daughter to become a prostitute (Leviticus 19:29):

> Do not prostitute your daughter, to cause her to be a harlot, lest the land fall to harlotry and the land become full of wickedness.

4. Women are free to become Nazirites, a specifically "sanctified" group (Numbers 6:2):

> Speak to the people of Israel, and say to them: When either man or woman shall separate themselves to vow a vow of a Nazirite, to separate themselves for *Adonai*. . . .

5. Barren women, while depressed and desperate, are not cast off by their husbands or the tribe. Widows are to be cared for by the whole society. Perhaps most importantly, in a society where women were sexual property, incest with daughters and daughters-in-law, as well as certain other female relatives, was strictly forbidden (Leviticus 18:9–15):

> The nakedness of your sister, the daughter of your father or daughter of your mother, whether she was born at home or born abroad, their nakedness you shall not uncover. The nakedness of your son's daughter, or of your daughter's daughter, their nakedness you shall not uncover; for theirs is your own nakedness. The nakedness of your father's wife's daughter, fathered by your father, she is your sister, you shall not uncover her nakedness. You shall not uncover the nakedness of your father's sister; she is your father's flesh. You shall not uncover the nakedness of your mother's sister; for she is your mother's flesh. You shall not uncover the nakedness of your father's brother: do not approach his wife; she is your aunt. You shall not uncover the nakedness of your daughter-in-law: she is your son's wife; you shall not uncover her nakedness.

6. The commandment to rest on the Sabbath applies equally to men and women (Exodus 20:8–10):

> Remember the Sabbath day, to keep it holy. Six days shall you labor and do all your work; but the seventh day is the Sabbath of *Adonai* your God; in it you shall not do any work, you, nor your son, nor your daughter, your manservant, nor your maidservant, nor your cattle, nor your stranger who is within your gates.

THE QUESTIONS

1. Juxtapose the biblical quotes that incline toward women as property with those that point to women as persons. Is there a balance? If so, what might this balance point to? If not, what do you think the Bible is struggling with? What do these quotes tell us about biblical society in general?

2. The question of women and power is a theoretical one as much as a practical one. Do we expect women in power to act, think, talk, and even dress like men in power—or do we want them to be "different" in their more powerful roles? Why, or why not? Can you describe a powerful woman and what makes her so? How does she differ from a powerful man?

3. Women in newly found positions of power need new role models, new visions of what power is and what it means. Do we accept the patriarchal definitions of dominion and control that power connotes, or form a new definition? Paula Cooey writes:

   > Power that transforms people and bonds them with one another in communities calls in question prevailing conceptions of power as an exercise in control, particularly political, social, and economic control. . . . Dynamic tension between an experience of transformation as empowering, on the one hand, and feelings of ambivalence towards power on the other hand, provides the possibility for critical affirmation and continued creativity. . . .[1]

   a) Use Cooey's quote to look at women as rabbis, synagogue presidents, or leaders of large Jewish organizations.
   b) Are there any biblical women you can cite who may have felt ambivalent toward power as control?
   c) We all know the abuses of power. Are there ever abuses of powerlessness?

3

Eishet Chayil:
"A Woman of Valor" as Paradigm

THE ISSUES

Many women feel ambivalent when they hear *Eishet Chayil,* "A Woman of Valor " (Proverbs 31:10–31), a poem of praise to the perfect woman. They assume it is about her role only as wife and mother. Or they have only heard it read at funerals and assume it is for the typical housewife. Or they resent what they see as superwoman imagery even in its ancient form.

In fact, "A Woman of Valor" presents, for its time, a very well-balanced portrait. The poem can be divided into three distinct sections: woman as wife and mother, woman as business manager and independent financial source, and woman as spiritual being.

The poem begins with the key phrase, "a woman of valor." *Chayil,* a word usually reserved for men, connotes physical strength or might, a person "at the height of [his or her] powers and capabilities."[1] We know the word *chayil* is used in modern Hebrew to mean "soldier," but elsewhere in *Tanach* it is used to describe men of strength, high character, moral bearing, and renown.[2] In choosing this word as the first description of our perfect woman, the poem is setting the reader up to see this woman in an extremely positive light. She is then praised as a family member, a beacon of hope and light to her husband. Yet in the second part, she is equally lauded for her business acumen, her ability to manage a field and sell its produce. When she appraises a field and then buys it, we wonder: How was she able to do this? With her own money? It never says she asked her husband, asked for permission, or borrowed money from another source. The third section of the poem extols her personhood, her inner strength and goodness. "Her children declare her happy," because she is a happy person, well rounded and content. She perceives that her work is good, because productive service and work *are* good, and she wants to be a part of that endeavor. She is beautiful in an inner, more spiritual way. The end lines of the poem are perhaps the most powerful anywhere, given that our own modern society still judges women on their outer beauty first. "Charm is deceptive and beauty short-lived; but a woman who fears God shall be truly praised." The Hebrew word for "charm" is *chein,* suggesting cuteness and a little-girl type of appeal. Such charm is *sheker*—a lie. Do not believe women when they feel the need to "put on" that adorable poutiness. And beauty? It is *hevel*—fleeting, a breath, illusion. Beautiful women are the result of cosmetics. The poem radically and clearly suggests that it is not outer beauty that men should seek, but the inner spirit of a woman. She reveres God, gives *tzedakah,* speaks kindly—that is the real beauty of women that men should seek. In its modern context, it is a poem that men recite to women, in praise of their excellence at home and in the world at large. But in its historical context, if we look at the verses that precede the poem, we see it is advice the mother of Lemuel is giving him on finding the perfect catch for a future wife. Thus it is also a poem about women reminding men to look beyond the physical to the spiritual.

Chapter 31 is not the only place in Proverbs where woman is defined by her roles. In Proverbs 18:22 we are told, "He who finds a good woman [wife] finds goodness and favor with *Adonai,*" and in Proverbs 19:14 we learn that a "wise woman" is "a gift from the *Adonai.*" However, Proverbs 9:13 warns us against a "foolish" woman, and Proverbs 21:19 tells us it is better to live in a desert than with an angry and dour woman. Seen also in that larger context, chapter 31 seems respectful of the fuller picture of what womanhood can mean.

This is not a one-dimensional woman, dusting around the house in an apron, with no head for business or worldliness. This woman is as complex as we are today, and perhaps just as conflicted about her multiplicity of roles. "A Woman of Valor" includes her role as wife and mother, as business woman, and as a woman of morality and goodness. It is here we see the paradigm—and the ambivalence—of the biblical portrait of woman as both necessary family keeper and yet central actor in ongoing history.

The poem begins with a rhetorical question, "A woman of valor—who can find?" but ends with a statement, "Many are valorous, but you excel them all." So such a wonderful woman is truly not hard to find but rather, you should "seek her out."

THE TEXTS

1. A traditional translation of Proverbs 31:10–31, *Eishet Chayil*, "A Woman of Valor":

> A woman of valor—who can find? Her price is far above rubies. Her husband has confidence in her, and so he has no lack of gain. She does him good and not evil all the days of her life. She seeks wool and flax, and works willingly with her hands. She is like the merchant ships; she brings her food from afar. She rises while it is still night, and gives food to her household, and a portion to her maidens. She appraises a field and buys it; with the fruits of her own hands she plants a vineyard. She girds herself with strength and performs her tasks with vigor, she sees that her business thrives, and her lamp goes on far into the night. She takes hold of the distaff, and her hands work the spindle. She stretches forth her palms to the poor and reaches forth her hands to the needy. She is not afraid of snow for her household; her whole household is clothed in scarlet. She makes coverlets for herself; all her clothing is fine linen and purple. Her husband is known in the gates, when he sits among the leaders of the land. She makes garments and sells them; she delivers girdles to the merchant. Strength and dignity clothe her, and she is cheerful about the future. She opens her mouth with wisdom, and words of kindness are on her tongue. She looks well to the ways of her household and does not eat the bread of idleness. Her children declare her happy; her husband sings her praises: "Many daughters are valorous, but you excel them all." Charm is deceptive and beauty short-lived; but a woman who fears God shall be truly praised. Give her from the fruit of her hands; let her own deeds praise her in the gates.

2. Another translation, by Susan Grossman, found in Ron H. Isaacs and Kerry M. Olitsky, *A Jewish Mourner's Handbook* (Hoboken, N.J.: Ktav Publishing House, 1991), 78:

> *A Woman of Valor*
>
> A good wife/who can find her
> she is worth far more than rubies
> she brings good and not harm
> all the days of her life
> she girds herself with strength
> and finds her trades profitable

wise counsel is on her tongue
and her home never suffers for warmth
She stretches her hands to the poor
reaches her arms to the needy
all her friends praise her
her family blesses her
she is known at the gates
as she sits with the elders
dignity, honor are her garb
she smiles at the future.

3. In that same book, on page 79, Grossman offers a "male version" of *Eishet Chayil,* in praise of a man. In it she modifies the
traditional text from Proverbs:

A good man who can find him
he is worth far more than rubies
never lacks for gain
he shares the household duties
and sets a goodly example
he seeks a satisfying job
and braces his arms for work
he opens his mouth with wisdom

he speaks with love and kindness
his justice brings him praises
he raises the poor, lowers the haughty.

4. Amy Bardack, "Praising the Work of Valiant Women: A
Feminist Endorsement of *Eshet Hayil,*" in *Lifecycles,* vol. 1,
Jewish Women in Life Passages and Personal Milestones, ed.
Debra Orenstein (Woodstock, Vt.: Jewish Lights, 1994), 138:

In the first nine chapters of the Book of Proverbs, wisdom is per-
sonified and deified as a woman. Numerous correlations between
Wisdom, who opens the Book of Proverbs, and the Valiant
Woman, who closes it, suggest that the authors and editors of
Proverbs drew a deliberate analogy between the two figures. . . .
The connection of the Valiant Woman with the figure of Wisdom
signifies that women, through their daily activities, exhibit the
shared human-divine characteristic of wisdom.

THE QUESTIONS

1. Parse the traditional translation into three sections. Which lines are praise of a family woman? Which of a business woman? Which of a moral woman? Do they balance out? Why are they spread out and not in three neat packages? Are there other categories of praise you find?

2. Notice that her husband is praised "in the gates." Why? What is the significance of the gates? Do you think she is famous because of him or he is famous because of her? What role does he seem to play in the poem?

3. Do you think of this woman as a "superwoman"? Does the poem set up unrealistic expectations? In what ways?

4. Rewrite "A Woman of Valor" for today. Choose three sections of importance to women in their roles and their lives today. What would those three sections be? Describe such a woman. Is there a "woman of valor" in your community who fits the interpretation offered in the introductory section?

5. Why do you think "A Woman of Valor" was written? To teach men about "real" women? To keep women "in their place"? To praise strong, unusual women? To provide women with role models? Or to help men fantasize about the perfect woman they may never have?

6. Compare the two translations. Which do you prefer, and why? Does Grossman's translation strengthen or soften the woman of valor?

7. Would you feel comfortable reciting a poem in praise of men at your Sabbath table? Why, or why not?

8. Do you agree with Bardack's assessment that women are associated with wisdom? Is there any danger to that association?

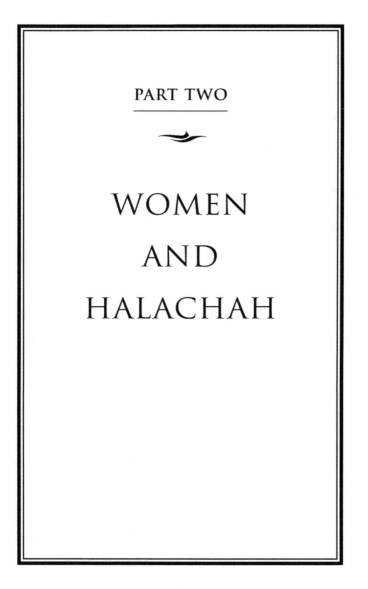

PART TWO

WOMEN
AND
HALACHAH

4

Time-Bound Mitzvot

THE ISSUES

In an article written in 1982, "God and Feminism," Judith Plaskow wrote:

> Of the issues that present themselves for attention, halacha has been at the center of feminist agitation for religious change . . . but while this issue has been considered and debated frequently in the last ten years, it is specific halachot that have been questioned and not the fundamental presuppositions of the legal system. . . . Underlying specific halachot, and *outlasting their amelioration or rejection* is an assumption of women's Otherness far more basic than the laws in which it finds expression.[1]

Many years later, we still spend a great deal of time questioning whether women may or may not, can or can not, should or should not do things like wear a *tallit,* wear a *kippah,* or count in a minyan. The major Jewish movements all deal differently with the questions of halachic authority. But whether you are in a halachic movement or a nonhalachic movement, there is no question that tradition, and the sense of history behind certain rituals and mitzvot, are fixed into our psyches. Even in egalitarian congregations, how many men do you see come up to light Shabbat candles? How many women lead the *Kiddush* around their tables at home?

Some women believe that changing halachah is the first step. If women are allowed to take synagogue leadership, wear ritual garb, and count in a minyan, they will change the face of organized Judaism. Others question whether halachic change should be part of the agenda only as a piecemeal solution—we can change this law but shouldn't change that one—or whether the entire halachic system should be recast to include women's voices and women's experience. Yet others posit a third option, doubting that any halachic change—whether piecemeal or whole—will change those assumptions upon which the laws are founded. The very fact that there exist any regulations at all that define women's roles, include or exclude women from any Jewish activity, prohibit or permit certain kinds of dress, speech, or behavior for women, or in any way categorize women suggests that women as a "class" are Other in the halachic system.

Some thinkers have even suggested that law itself is a male construct and a masculine way of maintaining a system, and thus they wonder whether any system of rules about men's and women's roles can ever be equalized.

Let us use the notion of "holiness" as an example. *Kadosh* is generally translated as "holy," but it can also mean "separate, different, apart." In the marriage vows, הרי את מקדשת לי *(harei at mikudeshet li . . .)* means both "behold you are sanctified to me" and also "you are set apart for me from other women/men." In the time of the Temple in Jerusalem, a sacrifice that was *hekdeish* was literally separated out from the rest of the herd. In Judaism, holiness is intrinsically linked to separateness, and the very heart of spirituality in Judaism is based on separation *(havdalah)* and on opposition: milk/meat, Shabbat/weekday, Jew/gentile, man/woman. What does this mean for women, taught from earliest childhood to be connected? What does this mean for those women who carry life inside, attached to, part of? What does this mean for those women who nurture and sustain from their very own bodies? What does this mean for women who form bonded friendships, taught from earliest memory to bring the family together, to be the cohesive force? Carole Gilligan, in her oft-quoted book *In a Different Voice,* studied the moral development of children.[2] She found that girls experience the world as a series of relationships; boys experience the world as a system of rules. Look at any schoolyard. If the boys play a game, the rules will win: "If you don't like it, get off the team!" But if girls play a game, the relationships win: "If you don't like it, well, then, we'll just play another game! We'll make up new rules!" The Jewish concept of spirituality, the Jewish attempt at communion with God, the Jewish quest for holiness, is rooted in adherence to rules, which we call mitzvot. Even Reform Judaism today works on the model of rules, albeit abridged; but the underlying concept of Judaism as adherence to rules has not yet been challenged. Can we redefine *k'dushah* as something other than separateness? Can we redefine mitzvot not as rules, but as dialogue, as action, as reaching toward?

Rachel Biale, in her book *Women and Jewish Law,* points out that in fact there are two kinds of "gender-specific" mitzvot.[3] There are those that, by biological necessity, dictate a different rule for men and for women. Men are prohibited in the Torah from shaving their side-locks. Women are commanded specifically around childbirth. Those mitzvot are biologically based. Within that context we may ask whether we would *want* all gender-specific mitzvot to be egalitarian. Would we want baby girls ritually circumcised in some way to be "equal"?

But then there are those mitzvot whose coding by gender seems more based on sociology. The social order of our ancestors imposed a strict boundary delineation between male and female behavior. Thus, for example, men were allowed to function as priests, women not. The law in Deuteronomy 22:5, which prohibits a man from wearing a woman's garment or a woman from putting on a man's clothing, best exemplifies this strict gender boundary. Wearing the other's clothes puts one in a "gray" area, blurs the boundaries, and gives access into the other's social system.

The Talmud attempts to formulate an easy and generalized criteria for which legal obligations should fall upon women and which upon men. That system is called *mitzvot aseh shehazman g'ramah,* time-bound mitzvot, from which women are exempt.

In the Talmud, mitzvot are divided by whether they can be performed at any time of day, or must be performed only at a certain time. Thus, for example, *t'fillin* may be put on only during the morning hours and are not put on in the evening; likewise, the *tallit* (the only exception is *Kol Nidrei*). Shabbat and *Yom Tov* candles are lit only in the evening. The morning *Sh'ma* and evening *Sh'ma* have time limitations. Those mitzvot that must be performed only at a certain time are called "time-bound mitzvot" or, in Hebrew, *mitzvot aseh shehazman g'ramah*—literally, "positive ['thou shalt'] mitzvot upon whom time depends," and from these, women are *p'turot,* "exempt." But women are not exempt from any positive mitzvah not dependent on time, and from any negative mitzvah ("thou shalt not") at all.

However, this rule is broken in several talmudic passages. Take Shabbat candles, for instance. Certainly the one mitzvah most associated with women is, indeed, time-bound! Yet women are most definitely not exempt from lighting Shabbat candles at their proscribed time. Eating matzah on Pesach is another example, though that mitzvah can only be performed during Pesach! Women are not exempt from lighting the Chanukah menorah, also time-bound, or from saying the Blessing after Meals, *Birkat HaMazon.* So while the Rabbis obviously felt strongly about exempting women in general, when it came to specific mitzvot, women were included, though this inclusion seems to "bend" the time-bound mitzvot rule.

The Talmud never gives a reason as to why women are exempt from these rituals and rites. The most common traditional suggestion is that women do not "need" external reminders of their relationship to God; their "inner rhythms" link them immediately to God. This, some have said, is not equally true of men, who need daily, and even hourly, obligations imposed upon them to maintain their spiritual connection. In addition, it has also been explained that because women are usually busy with an equally important mitzvah—raising children—the Rabbis were thus acting compassionately when they exempted women from having to be on their own at specific places at specific times.

But others believe this exemption is more political. Many of the time-bound mitzvot are public and involve religious leadership. They are acts that place the person in the public domain, a domain from which women were historically absent. Being in a minyan, reading from the Torah, building a sukkah, even circumcising a son, cause one to stand visibly in the public arena. Perhaps this exemption was meant to keep women out and men in?

And still others wonder why the exemption exists throughout a woman's life, and not just while she is raising a family. Unmarried women, for example, and young girls are still exempt from the performance of these mitzvot. Perhaps there is a social component, as well, leaving the institution where many of these mitzvot take place—the synagogue—in male hands.

THE TEXTS

1. Babylonian Talmud, *Kiddushin* 29a:

    Mishnah. All obligations of the son upon the father, men are bound, but women are exempt. But all obligations of the father upon the son, both men and women are bound. All affirmative precepts limited to time, men are liable and women are exempt. But all affirmative precepts not limited to time are binding upon both men and women. And all negative precepts, whether limited to time or not limited to time, are binding upon both ben and women; excepting, ye shall not round [the corners of your heads], neither shalt thou mar [the corner of thy beard], and, he shall not defile himself to the dead.

2. Some exceptions:
    a) Babylonian Talmud, *M'gillah* 4a:
       Said Rabbi Y'hoshua ben Levi: Women are obligated to read the *M'gillah,* because they too were part of the miracle.
    b) Babylonian Talmud, *P'sachim* 108b:
       Said Rabbi Y'hoshua ben Levi: Women are obligated to drink the four cups [of seder wine], because they too were part of the miracle.
    c) Babylonian Talmud, *Shabbat* 23a:
       Said Rabbi Y'hoshua ben Levi: Women are obligated to light the Chanukah lamps, because they too were part of the miracle.
    d) Babylonian Talmud, *B'rachot* 20b:
       Said Rava: Anyone who is bound by the Sabbath restrictions is similarly bound by the Sabbath ritual acts.
    e) Babylonian Talmud, *P'sachim* 43b:
       Said Rabbi Elazar: Women are obligated to eat matzah on Pesach, according to the Torah, for anyone who is bound not to eat *chameitz* is similarly bound to eat matzah.

3. One who is not obligated cannot lead one who is. Babylonian Talmud, *Rosh HaShanah* 29a:

    This is the general principle: one who is not himself under obligation to perform a religious duty cannot perform it on behalf of a congregation.

4. What if a woman obligates herself?

   a) Talmud, *Chagigah* 16b:

   Speak unto the sons of Israel . . . and he shall lay his hands [Leviticus 1:2–4, on the protocol for sacrificing animals]. The sons of Israel lay on the hands, but the daughters of Israel do not lay on the hands. Rabbi Yosei and Rabbi Shimon say: The daughters of Israel may lay on the hands optionally. Rabbi Yosei said: Abba Eleazar told me: Once we had a calf that was a peace-sacrifice, and we brought it to the Women's Court, and women laid the hands on it—not that the laying on of the hands has to be done by women, but in order to gratify the women [Or: to give them spiritual satisfaction, in Hebrew *nachat ruach*].

   b) *Shulchan Aruch, Yoreh Dei-ah* 246:6:

   A woman who has studied Torah has a reward but not as much as the reward of a man, because she is not commanded, and thus performs it of her own free will.

5. Many women in the Reform movement have taken on the mitzvah of wearing a *tallit,* and some have taken on putting on *t'fillin.*

   a) Dvora E. Weisberg, "On Wearing Tallit and Tefillin," in *Daughters of the King,* ed. Susan Grossman and Rivka Haut (Philadelphia: Jewish Publication Society, 1992), 283:

   I realize that wearing tallit and tefillin is a highly visible action and one that arouses strong emotions in other people. I know that what I intend to be my personal commitment becomes a public statement every time I enter a synagogue. While part of me responds to the opportunity to represent a change in women's patterns of observance, there is also a part that sometimes longs to be an unremarkable member of the congregation.

   b) Here is a personal account of what taking on a mitzvah usually done by males feels like to one woman, Elizabeth Tikvah Sarah (in *Taking Up the Timbrel,* eds. Sylvia Rothschild and Sybil Sheridan [London: SCM Press, 2000], 35–36):

Meditation for Tefillin

I cannot
bind myself

to You
I can only
unbind myself
continually and
free
Your spirit
within me
So why
this tender-cruel
parody of
bondage
black
leather
straps
skin
gut and
sacred litany of
　　power and
　　submission
which binds us
Your slave-people
still?
My own answer is
wound around
with every
taut
binding and
unbinding
blood rushing
heart pounding
life-force surging
pushing
panting
straining
struggling to
break through
to You

THE QUESTIONS

1. There is little agreement about what the word "exempt" means. Does it suggest women don't have to do these mitzvot, but should if they can? Or women don't have to do these, and therefore shouldn't? Weigh the argument for doing them against the halachic reasoning that the one who is commanded to perform is on a higher plane than the one who does so voluntarily. Why is this a higher plane?

2. Is there a common theme of those time-bound mitzvot from which women are exempt? Can you see a pattern in the exceptions to the rule? Why do you think the exceptions are there?

3. Comment on these explanations:
   a) Since women are busy raising children, and that is the ultimate mitzvah, they shouldn't be commanded to stop that mitzvah to perform another one, and so commanding them to be available at certain restricted times of the day is unfair, unkind, and unrealistic.
   b) Women don't "need" such mitzvot because they are already close to God because they give life.
      Are these explanations satisfying to you? What about the political answers—do they appeal to you? Add your own explanations. What are your guesses as to why the Rabbis exempted women from these mitzvot?

4. Read Elizabeth Tikvah Sarah's "Meditation for Tefillin." Have you ever taken on a new mitzvah? Was it a mitzvah traditionally done by males (e.g., Torah reading, wearing a *tallit,* leading *Kiddush*)? How did it feel? Did you ever feel "blood rushing, heart pounding" in the performance of a mitzvah? Why do you think Elizabeth Tikvah Sarah feels this way when she puts on *t'fillin*? Does it have something to do with being female, or perhaps is that the way we should feel with every mitzvah, even the ones done more typically by women, like lighting the Sabbath candles?

5

Blood and Water:
The Menstrual and *Mikveh* Laws

THE ISSUES

Judaism posits a healthy sexuality for both men and women. Put simply, sex is not "dirty," but it is regulated to certain times, certain places, and with certain people. Within those parameters, Judaism believes that sex is a holy act. Those parameters also require sex to be pleasurable for both the man and the woman. Within a heterosexual marriage, almost any kind of lovemaking is permitted to achieve that pleasure. A husband's marital responsibility includes his wife's sexual pleasure, so much so that a traditional marriage certificate, the *ketubah,* stipulates that the wife may expect regular and enjoyable sexual activity.

In modern Western thought, there is a division between mind and body. In such thought, body is bad and mind is good; God is symbolized as closer to mind, soul, or essence. "Godliness" means soul and therefore goodness. The absence of godliness means carnality and therefore evil. The Torah helps us reject this mind-body bifurcation, with its emphasis on the body as a symbol of God's creativity and its insistence of human responsibility for health and well-being. In the realm of menstruation and birth, women have the most potent possibility of seeing ourselves as *both* body and spirit, an integrated whole. If this is true, then the biblical terms "purity" and "impurity" strike a strange chord. Why do they play such a large role in the Torah's restrictions around women? Do these terms have such a negative connotation that there is no way for modern women to relate to them? The examination of some interpretations may help answer these questions.

First, blood and water are the physical stuff of life and are both connected to women. Both can symbolize life or death, birth or destruction. Females bleed predictably and cyclically once a month for most of their adult life, yet they do not die. A sack of water breaks and flows out of them, yet they do not die. In blood and water we give life and, except in rare cases, live ourselves. This may have seemed superhuman to our ancestors and inspired both respect and fear.

Second, as anthropologist Mary Douglas has written, " . . . all margins are dangerous. . . . Spittle, blood, milk, urine, feces or tears by simply issuing forth have transversed the boundary of the body"[1] The body, both the physical body and the communal body, that is, society, must have boundaries. Douglas suggests that the human body is a metaphor for society in all ways; its ambiguity is everyone's ambiguity, its borders are everyone's borders. Judaism is bound by this notion of borders and separations: milk and meat, Shabbat and weekday, sacred and profane. Judaism's centrality of bodily boundaries is also a focus on societal boundaries. The Torah responds to boundary-breaking substances with what anthropologists call "taboos." Taboos are the system by which certain objects or persons are set aside as either sacred or accursed. The word "taboo" itself has no negative connotation. It can be something that is so powerful that you may not touch it, or something so important that you must sacrifice it. All powerful things are, in a sense, taboo.

Third, in the Torah, bodily taboos revolve around emissions of semen and blood, or nearness to a corpse. Through ejaculation, menstruation, childbirth, and contact with a corpse, we see ourselves as dying and then living again. The man who ejaculates experiences the letting go of self in a total way, being brought to the brink. A woman who gives birth may say she feels like she was in "the other world" at transition. In the corpse's face we see our own. Although the Torah does not explicitly say so, there is a sense of awe at the mystery and power not only of the substances themselves, but of the human beings who release them.

Fourth, the Torah is concerned with repopulation, with being fruitful and multiplying. In that sphere, sexuality is the conduit for birth, and in the eyes of the Torah, sexual fluids need to be controlled in the same way that sexuality needs to be controlled, so that birth is achieved through holy means. In Genesis, God brings order into the chaos of Creation. In Leviticus, God brings order into the chaos of human sexual creativity. One of the primary intentions of the Torah is to call attention to the workings of our bodies as sexual beings and to help us navigate that tightrope. In the original Torah legislation, men and women stand equally on that tightrope.

Fifth, the mixed metaphor of mystery and power, contact and avoidance dominates the entire Torah's expressions around blood. Blood, which is to be avoided in the realm of eating and sex, is the same substance that atones for the community in the sacrificial cult, and binds the individual male child to the Israelite covenant through circumcision. The restrictions and boundaries around menstruation need to be seen in light of the entire biblical duality of blood as the core of both life and death. Every aspect of our experience has the potential to sanctify, but also to pollute. That which we value most has the power to both elevate and hurt us. Money, sex, power, all the things we desire, have the potential to act equally as sources of goodness or sources of evil. Remember, the life force that sustains us can also kill us.

According to the Torah one who discharges either substance, blood or semen, or any other undescribed substance from his or her sexual organs, is rendered ritually impure, in Hebrew *tamei*. For women, ritual impurity through menstrual blood has a second, specific word, *nidah*. This word is used to describe both the impurity and the woman who has it. The menstruating woman is separated from men, though not from other women and children. And men experiencing a bodily emission from their genitals are similarly segregated in one way or another.

Both males and females who have a genital emission cause "contagion," and any person or object that touches them becomes impure. The English translations of the words for these emissions and their consequences do not fully convey the nuances of the Hebrew words. *Tamei,* normally translated as "impure" or "unclean," has nothing to do with dirt. *Tahor,* translated as "clean" or "pure," is not about physical cleanliness. These are, rather, ritual states, which ascertain whether or not the person having an emission may approach the cultic center, that is, the Tabernacle. The menstrual flow or semen is never considered *physically* unclean in and of itself.

The original biblical system of impurity, along with its prohibitions, was directed at *all* those with discharges, both men and women. They were prohibited from approaching the holy district of the Temple, considered the place of God's Presence. But the destruction of the Temple in 70 C.E. caused a radical shift in Jewish life, which included a change of the focus of these purity laws. Without a Temple, without a center that could contract impurity, it made sense for most of the purity laws to fall into disuse. The Rabbis declare that, after the destruction of the Temple, the laws of purity for men were eliminated, but remained intact for women. Thus while there was parallelism in the Torah for men's and women's purity after emissions, the Rabbis remove that parallelism, making the purity laws relevant normally only to women. They argue that since the Temple was gone, such laws of who may approach the Tabernacle were thus rendered irrelevant. Since women did not approach the Tabernacle directly, the laws of ritual impurity still applied to them. The Temple, now gone, was replaced by the home as the center of Jewish life. The husband replaced the priest as the symbol of religious authority in the home. The notion that menstruation was a powerful symbol of life and death was slowly overtaken by ideas of female "pollution" and discomfort with the whole female bodily experience. Once about holiness and approach, life mixing with death, power and danger, menstrual laws now became about sexual relations with a husband.

The childbirth *nidah* rules are more perplexing. Of course, there can be no male parallel to giving birth. But a woman can give birth to either a boy or a girl. When a woman gives birth to a male child, she is *nidah* for seven days, exactly as with a normal discharge. She then remains *nidah* for an additional thirty-three days, days in which it is presumed she still has postpartum genital bleeding. If she gives birth to a girl, she is *nidah* for exactly double that amount of time.

There are many possible interpretations as to that doubling of postpartum impurity, but since the Torah does not explain it, they can only be guesses. Some suggest it was merely physical. It is suggested that after the birth of a girl there is a longer period of bleeding. Others note that the newborn girl will, someday in the future, also bleed. The new mother then is impure for herself and also for her daughter. The double period of time may also reflect apprehension and anticipation about the infant daughter's potential fertility. Or it may represent the need of the mother for extra time alone to bond with a daughter in a society that values sons much more.

Water functions in the Torah as the source of purification from the taboos of semen and blood. The *mikveh* is a small pool of "living water" about the size of a whirlpool tub, but without jets. The water must be part rainwater or water taken from a natural source, so that it is truly "living." Traditionally, those ready to change their existential status go to *mikveh* to mark that shift. You go into the water as one kind of person, you come out another. People converting to Judaism are initiated in the *mikveh.* Brides about to become married women go, before the wedding ceremony. Some grooms now go as well.

The *mikveh,* the pool of living waters, simulates an experience of drowning and then resurrection. About this experience at the *mikveh,* Aryeh Kaplan writes, "When a person immerses himself in water, he places himself in an environment where he cannot live. Were he to remain submerged for more than a few moments, he would die from lack of air . . . in a sense, the *mikveh* also represents the grave. . . . The representation of the *mikveh* as both womb and grave is not a contradiction. Both are places of non-breathing, and are end points of the cycle of life."[2]

Blood comes only from inside the body; it is produced there and has no outside source of its own. If we need more, we must get it from another body. Water is blood's symbolic partner but also its symbolic opposite. Though the human body is comprised of water, if we need more, we can go almost anywhere to find it. We cannot produce the water we need to live. We find its sources and there it is for us, drinkable, bathable, giving life to the faint and sick. It births us. It sustains us. But it is not truly *of us.* Lakes, rivers, and streams attest to creative powers outside of the human realm. Rain falls without our exertion, independent of our will. No wonder our ancestors, in their desert environment, chose water as the ultimate symbol of purity and purification. It transforms us because it is both in us and independent of us.

Water has an organic connection to women as the fluid of birth, for a baby floats in a sack of water inside its mother. Water also acquires a connection to women in the Torah, as each matriarch meets her husband at a well and as Miriam's life stories all take place around water. Thus the *mikveh,* the traditional pool or collection of living water used for immersions, can also be a symbol of rebirth for Jewish women.

THE TEXTS

1. Genesis 9:3–5:

   > Every creature that lives shall be yours to eat; just as with the plants I give you these. Except that flesh with its life-blood you shall not eat. For your own life-blood I will exact retribution [or: I will require a reckoning], for beast as well as human I will exact it. . . .

2. Leviticus 17:11:

   > For the life of the flesh is in the blood, and I have assigned it to you for expiation for your lives upon the altar; it is the blood, acting as life, that effects expiation.

3. Leviticus 15:2, 13:

   > When any man has an issue discharging from his sexual organ, he is ritually impure. . . . When one with a discharge becomes purified from the discharge, he shall count off seven days for the purification, wash his clothes, and bathe his body in "living water" and become ritually pure.

4. Leviticus 15:16, 19, 24–25, 28–30:

   > When a man has an emission of semen, he shall bathe his whole body in water and remain ritually impure until the evening. . . . When a woman has her discharge, it being blood from her body, she shall be considered a *nidah* [menstruant or put away] for seven days; whoever touches her shall be ritually impure until the evening. . . . If a man lies with her, her condition of *nidah* is upon him and he shall be ritually impure seven days, and any bedding upon which he lies is also impure. When a woman has had a discharge of blood for many days, not at the usual time of her menstruation [*nidah*], she shall be ritually impure like at the time of her *nidah,* as long as her discharge lasts, she shall be ritually impure. . . . When she is pure from her discharge, she shall count off seven days, and after that, she is ritually pure. On the eighth day she shall take two turtledoves or two pigeons, and bring them to the priest at the entrance to the Tent of Meeting. The priest shall offer the one as a sin offering and the other as a burnt offering, and the priest shall make expiation on her behalf for her ritually impure discharge. . . .

5. Leviticus 12:2, 4–5:

> When a woman at childbirth bears a male, she shall be ritually impure seven days; she shall be impure as at the time of *nidah*. . . . She shall remain in a state of blood purification for thirty-three days. . . . If she bears a female, she shall be ritually impure for two weeks as during *nidah,* and she shall remain in a state of blood purification for sixty-six days.

6. Rachel Adler, "In Your Blood, Live: Re-Visions of a Theology of Purity," in *Lifecycles,* vol. 2, *Jewish Women on Biblical Themes in Contemporary Life* (Woodstock, Vt.: Jewish Lights, 1997), 203, 205:

> The uncontrolled blood flowing from women's genitals is blood that has the power to contaminate. Its antithesis is the blood of circumcision deliberately drawn from men's genitals, which has the power to create covenant. . . . I do not believe the laws of purity will ever be reinstated, nor should they be. The worlds reflected in such rules are not the worlds we inhabit. Neither should we seek to replicate such worlds. They are unjust.

7. Rabbi Elyse Goldstein, *ReVisions: Seeing Torah through a Feminist Lens* (Woodstock, Vt.: Jewish Lights, 1998), 126:

> I am a Reform Jew, a rabbi and a feminist, and I go to the mikveh every month. For me, it is an experience of reappropriation, a rebirth: first of myself as a woman and a Jew, a regrounding after my period or after times of stress or upheaval; then a rebirth of the entire mikveh ritual itself. The mikveh has been taken from me by sexist interpretations . . . by a history of male biases, fears of menstruation and superstitions. I return each month to "take back the water."

THE QUESTIONS

1. Unlike the law of consuming the meat of sacrifices, which is restricted only to males (Leviticus 6:22), the prohibition against consuming blood is incumbent not only upon males but also upon females, not only Israelites but also non-Israelites. It is directed not only to priests, but to commoners, not only in the sacred precincts, but in all dwellings (Leviticus 7:26–27). Read the first two texts from Torah on the prohibition of eating blood. What reasons do they seem to suggest for the eating taboo? What qualities of blood make it taboo? In what ways are the eating and sexual taboos similar?

2. Think about all the places where blood plays a central role:
   a) The sacrificial system. Priests sprinkled it on the horns of the altar for cleansing and dedication, spread it on earlobes and toes for consecration of initiates, dashed it around the altar itself. It is regularly poured on the ground and covered with earth, moved away or hidden.
   b) Blood saves the people in Exodus. The lamb's blood smeared on the doorposts of the Israelites saves their firstborn from destruction on the night of the first Passover.
   c) *B'rit milah.* In the covenant of circumcision, the *dam b'rit,* literally "covenantal blood," is central.
      Contrast these central roles to the central role of blood in the menstrual laws. Where are there similarities, and where are there differences? What role does blood play symbolically and practically in each?

3. Is there any positive expression of separation from men during menstruation we can take on? Does separation ever have an elevating aspect to it? Why or why not?

4. Is there a Jewish quality we can ascribe to a woman's *b'rit* of blood? What if menstrual blood was *dam b'rit*—covenantal blood—for women? What if girl children were named at eight days or at birth, but formally brought into the covenant at men-

struation with a Jewish rite? What would a woman's *b'rit* menstrual ceremony look like? What about menopause? What kind of ceremony, if any, should mark the end of menstruation?

5. Read Adler and Goldstein and compare their views. Can we truly reappropriate *mikveh* from a feminist perspective, or is it an unjust system that should not be reinstated? What is your opinion about the new interest in *mikveh* in the non-Orthodox Jewish communities? Where might it be coming from, and where might it lead? Should we be working toward a new definition of *mikveh* now, or is it just too steeped in sexist notions? Should we be looking to a new ritual to fill the meaning that *mikveh* might have originally had?

6. What do you think "taking back the waters" means? Is that politicizing the *mikveh* too much? Or perhaps making it more relevant to today's young feminists? Imagine your synagogue is building a brand new *mikveh* for your members. What would it look like? How would it function? How would it be different from, or similar to, traditional *mikvaot*?

6

~

Rosh Chodesh

THE ISSUES

Modern Jewish women have found new meaning in the association of women and the moon. Rosh Chodesh, the new month, has become popular as a time for special ceremonies and special groups. These groups often meet on the Jewish new moon, which is actually the darkest day of the month, the night before the first sliver of new moon appears! The Hebrew "new moon" is, in fact, the "no moon." They create special rituals and celebrate time and space together. They may study and mark the connections between women and the moon, between menstrual cycles and the moon's cycles, and between the ancient symbols of the moon and the symbols of femininity. Theses modern links actually have ancient origins.

Early civilizations saw the moon as having influence over fertility, and worshiped it as a deity. The full moon, offering new hope and new life, was signaled with shouts and blasts of joy by royal trumpets. The waning moon represented the powers of destruction and death. Ancient societies equated the monthly cycle of women with the monthly cycle of the moon, and its swelling as a symbol of pregnancy.

Yet the Hebrew new month, also heralded by shofar blasts, takes place not on the full moon but on the last day of the old month, and, on a two-day Rosh Chodesh, also the first day of the new month. The ancient Hebrews blessed the moon at its darkest period, when its power is least evident, when it was specifically *not* worshiped by other cultures, when its femaleness, swelling, fullness, roundness are absent.

Our ancestors were familiar with both sun and moon cults. Sun cults, proliferating in Egypt and thus something our ancestors had seen and known, were in the hands of men. The Hebrews specifically and purposely rejected those sun cults and their association with Egypt by counting the Hebrew calendar not by the sun, but by the moon. In doing so, they acknowledged the powerful emotional tug of the feminine element in time. Ancient moon cults were generally in the hands of women, and Hebrew women would have been familiar with the reverent associations of the moon and femininity. In fact, in biblical days, so important was Rosh Chodesh that it had a special status like that of Shabbat, with special sacrifices and pageantry. In Numbers 10:10 we read, "Also, in the days of your gladness, and in your appointed seasons, and in your new moons, you shall blow the trumpets over your burnt offerings, and over the sacrifices of the burnt offerings; and they shall be for you a memorial to your God: I am *Adonai* your God." In rabbinic times, the sighting of the new moon was vitally important, for it was crucial that all the Jewish communities both in Israel and scattered in the Diaspora observe the coming holiday on the same day, for the holidays were based on the date of the new moon. Therefore an elaborate system of sighting, testifying to the sighting, and announcing the sighting was developed in the Mishnaic period. The sighting was relayed to distant communities by the use of fires and runners.

The later Rabbis find a midrash to explain, make acceptable, and Judaize the already acknowledged pagan connection of women and the moon. In effect, through this midrash, they authorize women to celebrate what they probably had already been celebrating anyway. According to *Pirkei D'Rabbi Eliezer,* a rabbinic midrash compiled in the eighth century C.E., women were rewarded with Rosh Chodesh for refusing to participate in the building of the Golden Calf. Even today Rosh Chodesh is, for Orthodox women as well as those not

Orthodox, a women's holiday on which women are commanded to rest and rejoice.[1]

Her followers called the moon goddess the goddess of renewal. She dies and is reborn, as women are renewed each month. Prayers to her for renewal are still intoned by Native peoples of the Americas. In the Jewish prayer book, it is God who renews the moon, and not the moon who renews herself. But as it says in the prayers for Rosh Chodesh, "in the time to come, they [humankind] will be renewed like it."[2] The word for month, in fact, has the same root as the word for "new"—*chadash*.

Rosh Chodesh represents an authentically Jewish practice that has been successfully reappropriated by Jewish feminists. It gives us an opportunity to see ourselves as linked to other women, to our menstrual cycles, to nature, and to history all at the same time. As Robin Zeigler writes, "Rosh Chodesh, as the waxing and waning of the moon, speaks to my feminine tasks. I must remind myself that my life is filled with constant change. My body . . . is constantly changing. My reality is to learn to live with these changes—to ebb and flow with them. . . ."[3]

THE TEXTS

1. Susan Weidman Schneider, *Jewish and Female: A Guide and Sourcebook for Today's Jewish Woman* (New York: Simon and Schuster, 1985), 95:

   > Celebrations of Rosh Chodesh have gained great popularity among women exploring Jewish rituals and spirituality and looking for something equally appropriate to women but fully within the Jewish tradition. . . . The rediscovery of Rosh Chodesh . . . is an example of the blending of a piece of traditional Judaism with women's present needs. The fact that the holiday does come out of the tradition brings women's observations of it into mainstream Judaism and out of the category of what some might consider mere invention.

2. Susan Weidman Schneider, *Jewish and Female: A Guide and Sourcebook for Today's Jewish Woman* (New York: Simon and Schuster, 1985), 96:

   > Though many Jewish feminists speak of Rosh Chodesh as a beautiful opportunity to use expressive ritual that is removed from the male-symbol world of the synagogue, other women disagree. . . . "A big deal—a holiday that has not much significance in the range of Jewish celebrations, so the women have to get it. We get to have a ceremony late in the day—a half holiday is all that it is officially. After we've cleaned the whole house, fed everybody, then we get to have a little holiday all to ourselves. The men have thrown us a little bone."

3. Jane Litman, Judith Glass, and Simone Wallace, "Rosh Chodesh: A Feminist Critique and Reconstruction," in *Celebrating the New Moon,* ed. Susan Berrin (Northvale, N.J.: Jason Aronson, 1996), 24:

   > Rosh Chodesh is not the appropriate reward for women's refusal to worship the golden calf. Justice would suggest that women's loyalty be rewarded with priestly power and leadership. . . . But no, the patriarchal story "gives" women what they already had!

4. *Pirkei D'Rabbi Eliezer* 45:

> The women heard about the construction of the Golden Calf and refused to submit their jewelry to their husbands. Instead they said to them, "You want to construct an idol and a mask which is an abomination, and has no power of redemption? We won't listen to you." And the Holy One rewarded them in this world in that they would observe the New Moons more than men, and in the next world in that they are destined to be renewed like the moon.

5. *Kitzur Shulchan Aruch* (Code of Jewish Law), vol. 2, chap. 97, #3, "Laws concerning Rosh Chodesh":

> Work is permissible on Rosh Chodesh. Women, however, customarily refrain from work on that day. It is a beautiful custom, and we should not make light of it.

THE QUESTIONS

1. Read the midrash upon which Rosh Chodesh as a woman's holiday is based. Is it convincing? What does it say about our biblical ancestors—both male and female—to you? Read the midrash after reading the story of the Golden Calf in Exodus 32. Do you think the midrash is believable? Based on what in the text?

2. Read Schneider's first quote. If Rosh Chodesh is so important and women have brought it into mainstream Judaism, why do you think it is still so unknown except in small circles? Why has it traditionally fallen into disuse, only to be resurrected by women's groups? Do you know any women who regularly celebrate it on their own and not through a group? How do they celebrate?

3. Read Schneider's second quote and the Litman et al. quote. Do you agree or disagree? Is Rosh Chodesh perhaps a "little bone" being thrown to women to satisfy them and get them to "stop complaining"? Should we reappropriate it and aggrandize it or look to larger celebrations? Should women have a holiday of their own at all? Why or why not?

4. Read the halachic text about how women should celebrate Rosh Chodesh. Do you know anyone who does? What elements of this celebration might you take into your own life? Why do you think it says "it is a beautiful custom, and we should not make light of it"?

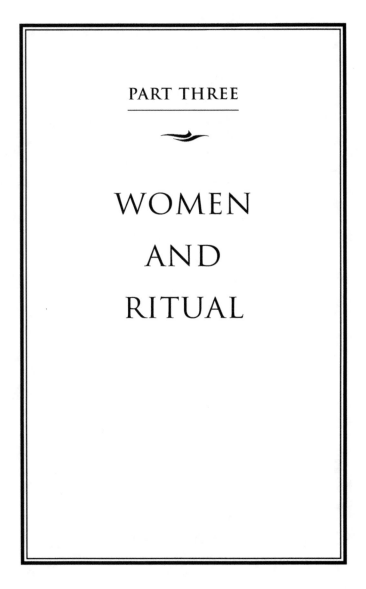

PART THREE

WOMEN
AND
RITUAL

7

~

Inventive or Imitative?

THE ISSUES

When women take on traditionally male rituals or roles, they often feel strange or awkward. One reason is unfamiliarity. Another is the reaction of the community around them. The third is the question of whether such rituals or roles have caused those women to be in imitation of men, or whether it has caused them to invent something completely new.

Jewish leaders today are continually facing the challenge of adapting age-old traditions to a more contemporary reality affected by feminism. At the same time, they are also being asked to create new rituals to fill the void where an absence is palpable—around birth, fertility and infertility, menstruation and menopause, and growing old. The upsurge of interest in spirituality has deeply affected all segments of the Jewish community, and often women in the rabbinate are thought of as "experts" in this growing field of the creation and adaptation of ritual for women. *Mikveh* ceremonies for miscarriage, rape, chemotherapy, and midlife milestones are being written and shared through personal contacts or word of mouth. Covenantal rituals for baby girls, more creative than the baby namings of old, are spreading. Yet, some people experience moments of ambivalence around these creative, invented ceremonies because they seem unconnected to much of Jewish history and shared experience.

Rituals provide a marking, a delineation, a framework of meaning around normal events. Rituals turn events that at first glance appear to be mundane into moments of sacred time because they are in fact so universal, so predictable, and so cyclical. For example, everyone somehow gets born. The vast majority of those who live to young adolescence reach puberty. In most cultures, people marry or form permanent relationship bonds that create families. Everyone dies. Participation in a birth ritual, a puberty ritual, or a death ritual not only frames this otherwise normal experience, but it defines the experience; in essence, the ritual *creates* the experience. A *b'rit milah* is a *defining* ritual. It reframes the perception of the birth of a baby boy from a physical moment in time to a reenactment of the ancient covenant between God and Abraham. Standing under a *chuppah* at a wedding is a *defining* ritual. It identifies the couple as standing under the roof of their newly created Jewish home and is a reenactment of the first wedding or coupling—of Adam and Eve. Thus in Judaism not only do rituals create experience by separating and marking moments, they also serve to create experience *in the participants* by moving them from the realm of "spectators" to the realm of "actors." The baby boy is Abraham. The couple are Adam and Eve. This is achieved not through theories and theologies but through actual drama. Perhaps the best example is the Passover seder, when we reexperience the bitterness of slavery through the rituals of eating *maror, charoset,* and matzah. We reexperience our slavery by acting it out in very specific ways.

So we must ask—when do women function as actors in this historical drama? How is a woman's life framed and defined through ritual? How is a woman's experience expressed in Jewish ritual?

We have certainly passed the first stage in answering these questions. Baby namings and egalitarian weddings are the norm and no longer the exception. Bat mitzvah is almost standard practice, and some form of it has been accepted in even the most traditional communities.

Now that women are so involved in adapting and imitating traditional ritual, the question is, do we also need to invent new ritual? In the past we have encouraged *imitative* ritual. In imitative ritual we redesign the traditional model by imitating it with a female twist. Thus a *tallit* created for a girl looks like a traditional *tallit* except in color, material, size, or specific design. It may have flowers or rainbows instead of black stripes. It may have lace or be made of silk instead of wool. But it is still a square or rectangular shawl with fringes on the end. In other words, we take the model of *tallit* and "feminize" it. A bat mitzvah still includes the traditional rubrics— the girl reads from the Torah, writes a speech, has a party. A baby naming looks like a *b'rit milah,* but without the cutting. This is imitative ritual, and it answers a deep need to equalize and normalize women's participation. It is easier, and less shocking, to see a woman in a traditional *tallit* and *t'fillin* than in a floor-length *tallit*-poncho with *t'fillin* made of ribbons and velvet.

But *inventive* rituals are different. How will they be uniquely our own? Will they include men? Will they focus on our biological womanhood—menstruation, childbirth, lactation—or a more inner sense of womanhood, not defined by physicality?

To be sure, imitative rituals can be extremely meaningful and satisfying. They fulfill the need for balance. They address the exclusive maleness of so much of our traditional life-cycle events. They normalize the entrance of women into the public religious life of the community. They make the tradition confront the spiritual need of women and include women on every level into the dramatic and sacred moments of life.

But on another level, imitative rituals are not satisfying. They say nothing of women *as women.* They do not mark the unique moments that happen only to women. They do not bond women with other women in a historical way. We do not know how women would have answered the question "How shall we mark this moment?" when many of these rituals were in their infancy. Inventive rituals are the beginning of an answer to the question of how to mark the moments of *women's* lives.

Inventive rituals reimagine. They start from scratch, having no historical bounds or expectations, no communal sanctions or communal standards. They ask, "Is there something uniquely female about this act, about this object?" By definition, they are not traditional. There is no ritual to imitate, for example, for first menstruation, for menopause, for lactation and weaning; for pregnancy, infertility, miscarriage; for children leaving home, for hysterectomy, for mastectomy; for rejoining the workforce after spending years at home, or for caring for an elderly parent. There simply may have to be new rituals in order to mark not only the significant transitions in our lives as women, but also the unique moments in women's experience, the drama of womanhood, women's perceptions of ritual, women's specific gifts, outlooks, and ways of seeing the world.

But inventive rituals are risky. They are not linked to thousands of years of practice. They do not look like what your grandmother did. A menstruation ceremony, a menopause *mikveh* celebration, a silk and appliqué *tallis*-cape with hood does not look or feel familiar. One ceremony does not necessarily link to the next, as Purim links to Pesach, as bar mitzvah links to *chuppah*. And we miss the knowledge that every other Jew in history and at this time is doing this ritual or marking this event.

Another risk is that new rituals may "divide and conquer" women into those with children and those without. They may make us seem very different from one another, based on whether or not we have experienced childbirth. Since many new rituals center around pregnancy and family, they often assume heterosexuality or heterosexual marriage and childbearing as the norm; thus they may exclude barren women or women who choose not to have children and women who do not marry. We will need to be open to the many faceted ways of being female, so that we do not fall into the trap of defining ourselves as mainly child bearers, child rearers, and caregivers.

How will we make these new rituals feel authentically Jewish so that, while they are not bound to a long history (your ancestors probably didn't do any of them!), they speak deeply to us as Jews, not only as feminists. To make them feel Jewish we will have to probe into the meaning of authenticity. Why does a *tallit* look the way it does? What makes any ritual authentic?

Sometimes inventive rituals work, but sometimes they do not. We should not have to grade them after only one generation and, if they fail, reject them. Rather, we should be able to keep building and experimenting, creating and discarding. Thus, women and ritual is a new and wide-open terrain, and in this sense we are still defining as we go.

THE TEXTS

1. Judith Plaskow, *Standing Again at Sinai: Judaism from a Feminist Perspective* (San Francisco: Harper and Row, 1990), 89:

   The real challenge of feminism to Judaism emerges, not when women as individual Jews demand equal participation in the male traditions, but when women demand equality as Jewish women, as a class that has been up until now seen as Other. . . . When women, with our own history and spirituality and attitudes and experiences, demand equality in a community that will allow itself to be changed by our differences, when we ask that our memories become part of the Jewish memory and our presence change the present, then we make a demand that is radical and transforming. Then we begin the arduous experiment of trying to create a Jewish community in which difference is neither hierarchalized nor tolerated but truly honored. Then we begin to struggle for the only equality that is genuine.

2. Sylvia Rothschild, "Expanding the Borders of Prayer," in *Taking Up the Timbrel,* ed. Sylvia Rothschild and Sybil Sheridan (London: SCM Press, 2000), 11:

   To begin with, when developing new liturgy or ritual, one must create the awareness of community and of place. For any prayer or ritual to have meaning, it must operate with the active co-operation of people who have come for a known reason, who are focused on explicitly stating that reason, who are able and willing to work together in the presence of God. . . .

3. Rabbi Debra Orenstein, introduction to *Lifecycles,* vol. 1, *Jewish Women on Life Passages and Personal Milestones* (Woodstock, Vt.: Jewish Lights, 1994), xxi–xxii:

   a) Rituals are "created" in at least three ways: By recovering traditions that have fallen into disuse, by using an existing rite or blessing in a new context, or by drawing on traditional texts, symbols, images, and ritual objects to create an entirely new composition. The first two methods renew the old creatively, while the last creates the new authentically. . . .

   b) More important than notions of subjectivity or relativity, however, is the social assessment of familiarity. In contemporary

Western culture, familiarity commonly does breed contempt. What is most available and most used is considered least interesting and essential. This contrasts sharply with the traditional Jewish emphasis on sanctifying the everyday. . . .

THE QUESTIONS

1. Using Plaskow's quote, what do you think the biggest challenges are in creating new ritual? Are you more comfortable creating new rituals or readapting old ones? Why? Use the birth of a baby girl, bat mitzvah, first menstruation, and funerals as examples.

2. Using Rothschild's quote, talk about a ritual (either specifically woman-centered or not) you attended or led that was "successful" in your mind. What made it so? What were the key elements? What makes a ritual "work" for you?

3. With which of Orenstein's three ways of creating ritual are you most comfortable? Can you enumerate any other ways? What do you think categorizes the "new authenticity"? What criteria would you use for a new ritual to be "authentic"?

4. Comment on Orenstein's second quote about familiarity. Are there some Jewish rituals that would fall under the heading of "familiarity breeds contempt" for you? Or does the familiarity of certain Jewish rituals always signal comfort?

5. In groups of twos or threes, develop a "new" ritual for women for a life event not already ritualized. What elements would be important? What would the goal of the ceremony be? Would both men and women participate? How would you develop the liturgy? Would you need new ritual symbols? What might they be?

6. In groups of twos or threes, take a traditional ritual and adapt it for women. If you were "in charge" of creating a ceremony for newborn girls based on the traditional *b'rit milah,* how would it look? What about a bat mitzvah, based on bar mitzvah?

8

~

Is Biology Spiritual Destiny?

THE ISSUES

First menstruation. Menopause. The beginning and end of a woman's menstrual cycle mark her days. Waiting for it to begin. Waiting for it to end. Trying not to get pregnant. Trying to get pregnant. There is no doubt that the menstrual cycle, pregnancy, childbirth or adoption, lactation, and menopause all mark a woman's life in a different way than any man's life is marked. There is also no doubt that while the Torah has clearly enunciated laws around a woman's sexual behavior at those times, there have been no ceremonial markers of those "life-cycle" moments—at least none that have made it down to us.

In the modern Jewish community, new ceremonies to mark those events have been discussed and are being tried. In the past few years, several new books have been published that detail such ceremonies (see bibliography). It is no longer a surprise to hear of a ceremony for weaning (based on the biblical precedent of the weaning ceremony of Sarah and Isaac in Genesis 21:8) or a ceremony for menopause. But these rituals are idiosyncratic. They are generally marked by the celebrants privately in their own homes, among their own friends, or in their small circle of extended family in their synagogue. They rarely enjoy community-wide recognition the way a wedding or a bar mitzvah is hailed as an achievement for more than just the immediate family. If a boy has a bar mitzvah in Idaho, I know more or less what it will look like. If a girl has a first menstruation ceremony in San Francisco, I have no idea if it will look like the one I saw in New Jersey or something completely different than I have ever imagined. While there is an abundance of creativity possible on this new model, there is also the danger of experimentation that ends up looking either trivial or extremely personal.

A case in point is the "baby-naming" ceremony, different from congregation to congregation, from family to family. In some synagogues the rabbi names the baby girl on a Friday night or a Saturday morning in front of the open ark. In others, the rabbi and the parents write a creative service, performed in their home on either the eighth day (to parallel a *b'rit milah*) or within thirty days. In yet other places, a girl is named by her own relatives at home, at any convenient time, with no rabbi as officiant. The service is not yet fixed and is still open and changing. Which rubrics, prayers, and blessings "must" you have at a baby naming? And do you give the name, or do you confer some covenantal status upon the child, as at a *b'rit?*

Baby namings for girls began as a way to make an egalitarian point. The birth of a girl in the Jewish community is no less a cause for celebration than that of a boy. Yet many other moments of our lives go ritually unmarked: first menstruation, pregnancy, lactation, menopause. Those moments speak of our lives *as women,* not only as Jews.

So should there be rituals to mark the biologically based moments of women's lives? This spirituality centers on our bodies, on our intuition, and on our connection with nature and the moon. On the one hand, it gives women a clear and positive message about our bodies, a message women desperately need in this society, which encourages self-negation and self-hatred for women's bodies. The high occurrence of eating disorders in women attests to the spiritual malaise many women feel about their physical selves. Never quite good enough, we are always too short, too fat, not just right physically. Rituals that celebrate the female body would do a great deal to turn a tide of negativity around.

These ceremonies also point to a reality in Judaism that is critical: there is no bifurcation between the spirit and the body, no Western split between holiness and physicality. There is no negation of the importance of a healthy, well-functioning, and even attractive body in Judaism. And while the focus of the genitals in Judaism is for procreation, there is no "dirtiness" or shame attached to our physical sexuality. Erich Fromm has called rituals "a system of symbolic behavior." If this is true, what is the symbolic behavior we wish the community to have around women's bodies? How can we affect this behavior through the use of ritual?

But on the other hand, these rituals do not speak of defining moments *as Jews:* the covenant with Abraham, the first reading of the Torah. Most women menstruate, not just Jewish women. These rituals also do not share other traditional modes of Jewish spirituality: the larger community of Jews, connection with agriculture, connection with history. These biological moments are private moments, not meant to be played out on a public stage. They do not speak of a collective unity; they speak rather of the individual in direct and private relationship with God. As such, they are a new and modern expression of an individualism historically undervalued in Jewish communal life. Rituals are meant to structure both space and time in a universalistic and communal way for all Jews. A child becomes a bar or bat mitzvah within a community, taking his or her place among the community's potential leaders. A baby is covenanted to the whole people Israel, and to God. As the seventh day is Shabbat and the ark contains the Torah, there are universal givens, which are not dependent on any one individual or family.

And what of the woman who, for whatever reason, does not menstruate? What of the man who takes an active role in the birthing and parenting of his child? What of the mother who does not breastfeed? What of the infertile couple? What of the individual who does not fit into any stereotypical gender definition? Critics of biologically based rituals point out that such gender-specific ceremonies like menstruation, pregnancy, lactation, or weaning ceremonies shut men—including our own sons—out of some of the most important moments in their family life. Such ceremonies form bonded communities of women that may exclude men or may exclude women who do not fit into a stereotypical mold of wife and mother. Is the spirituality of a woman somehow "coded" so that she finds the most fulfillment in her role of mother? What about those who do not?

But perhaps the largest question in regard to biologically based rituals is, how do we validate and celebrate the unique aspects of being female without reducing ourselves—as we have been reduced by others in the past—to being wombs and breasts and baby producers, gender-coded in societally rigid ways? How do we celebrate potentially sacred moments without trivializing and condensing them to their earthly physicality (blood, milk, etc.)? And how do we acknowledge ourselves as physical, female beings while also holding fast to ourselves as Jews?

THE TEXTS

1. Debra Orenstein, introduction to *Lifecycles,* vol. 1, *Jewish Women on Life Passages and Personal Milestones* (Woodstock, Vt.: Jewish Lights, 1994), xxii:

> Some people fear that the proliferation of rituals around women's biological cycle will reinforce the notion that women are linked to earth and body, and men to mind and God. If women want some of their most private biological moments to be addressed and recognized by the community, however, that hardly means that they want *only* their biological needs to be addressed and recognized. Moreover, biology and spirit are at bottom inseparable, particularly . . . in such momentous passages as childbirth, miscarriage, abortion, and menopause.

2. Debra Orenstein, introduction to *Lifecycles,* vol. 1, *Jewish Women on Life Passages and Personal Milestones* (Woodstock, Vt.: Jewish Lights, 1994), xx:

> Traditional religious ritual was designed, and continues, to meet a variety of needs that relate to life passages: The need for the individual to be acknowledged by community, the need for the community/tribe to read itself into the passages of each member, the need for bonding, which serves both individual and community, the need to (re)enact dramatically the great stories and messages of the tradition. . . . Through rituals, we create structures that provide an element of predictability, and therefore, safety, around times of insecurity, transition, and/or loss.

3. Shonna Husband-Hankin, in *Celebrating the New Moon,* ed. Susan Berrin (Northvale, N.J.: Jason Aronson, 1996), 103:

> *New Moon–First Moon Celebration:*
> *Welcoming Daughters into the Circle of Women*
>
> On Rosh Chodesh evening, a few days after her first period began, we gathered around our table. Candles were lit, and the Shecheyanu blessing was recited in the feminine form. We each took turns, ushering into our circle the names of mothers, grandmothers, and other women friends. Each person offered a flower, one by one interweaving it into a braided fabric "crown" I had made, which was then placed on Talya's head.

A special kiddush cup was filled with deep, red raspberry and grape juice, fruits of the vine. Around the circle the "simcha cup" was passed, a sacred goblet that has been used at over a hundred Jewish life-cycle ceremonies among our community of extended friends. As each girl or woman held the cup, they offered their own unique blessing for Talya's blossoming. And together we chanted the Hebrew blessing over the fruit of the vine.

A ritual pouch was filled with individual offerings for the newly menstruating young woman, including gifts of seashells, crystals, earrings with moons, and angel cards. Songs and drums filled the air, and stories were shared by those who had gone before on this path to womanhood. . . . As her mother, I said a few words and offered a special prayer. I also, at that time, gave her a new (middle) name to pass on the female lineage in our family. . . . We closed with a silent prayer and a song. Finally, we shared ritual treats to eat: many seeded fruits as fertility symbols, crescent moon cookies, lush dates and figs, and deep red juices.

THE QUESTIONS

1. Read Orenstein's first quote. Can you articulate what the critics of biologically based rituals would say? Do you agree with those criticisms? Why or why not?

2. Read Orenstein's second quote. How can we create specifically biologically based rituals that answer the general criteria of good ritual? Are there some biological passages that simply cannot or do not "deserve" ritual recognition? Communal recognition? "Through rituals, we create structures that provide an element of predictability, and therefore, safety, around times of insecurity, transition, and/or loss." Can biologically based rituals provide those elements? How?

3. Read the menstruation ceremony created by Shonna Husband-Hankin for her daughter. What elements of that ritual seem familiar? Which ones seem new? Does the ceremony resonate with you? Could you imagine doing this or a similar ceremony? Do you see any danger in such a ceremony? Do you think such a ceremony will help or hinder young Jewish girls in their spiritual development?

4. In groups of twos or threes, choose a biologically based life passage for women and create a ritual for it. Who would come? What would be the elements? Where would it be held? Base your ritual on the criteria noted in Orenstein's second quote. Where does it fall short? Where does it succeed?

9

Women and the Synagogue

THE ISSUES

Traditional Judaism exempts women from public, time-bound prayer, such as saying the morning *Sh'ma* at a certain hour or counting in a minyan. However, there is no indication that women shouldn't pray or that God "feels" differently about the prayers of women. Indeed the Talmud obligates women to say the Blessing after Meals and to recite the *Amidah* prayer. The very notion of the importance of prayer and the model of prayer itself, in fact, come from a woman. Hannah's prayer in I Samuel 2 is understood as a model of perfect supplication. But because women are not obligated in the same way men are, and because of the general principle that one who is not obligated cannot fulfill a mitzvah for one who is, in traditional Judaism women neither count in nor lead a minyan. A minyan must be made up of ten people who share the same level of obligation. That is why, for example, even in egalitarian congregations neither children nor gentiles count in a minyan, though women do.

The same goes for wearing a *kippah* or *tallit*. Although traditional Judaism exempts women from these mitzvot because they are "time bound" it has become the norm in many congregations, across the denominational spectrum, to see women in a varied array of prayer garments and donning *t'fillin*. Although this feels like an innovation, the Talmud records a discussion concerning Michal, daughter of King Saul, who put on *t'fillin,* and no one stopped her (Babylonian Talmud, *Eiruvin* 96a), and so even the early Rabbis recognized that there must be women who desire to perform the mitzvot of *tallit* and *t'fillin.* Those two rituals raise the question of both the halachah against women's wearing a man's garment and the notion of women's exemption from time-bound mitzvot, but many women, even in the Orthodox community, are exploring what the taking on of those mitzvot might mean for them. Certainly societal dictates of what is "men's fashion" or "women's fashion" are not timeless and have changed through the centuries. We know that in ancient days men wore long robes, similar to the Bedouin Jalabeahs of today! Some feel strongly that to don a *tallit* or put on *t'fillin* is imitation of men's ritual, while others feel that doing so is in keeping with the notion of egalitarianism in liberal Judaism. Either way, prayer garments do play a strong spiritual role in the worshiper's experience. They separate you from your normal dress, mark the moment as a prayerful one, and often help in spiritual preparation for prayer. As women choose to wear these prayer garments, they are also answering the question "why?" Why should a woman take on this ritual or, in fact, any ritual that has until now been seen as belonging in the male domain? Are we trying to be honorary men or trying to be closer to God? To be better Jews, better feminists, or both?

Prayer garments are only one aspect of synagogue life. Before we can explore the question of the role of women in the synagogue, we should define the role of the synagogue in our lives altogether. Is the synagogue central, or is the Jewish home central, or both?

Before the destruction of the Temple in Jerusalem in 70 C.E., Jewish ritual life concentrated on one central address. Animal sacrifices and priestly ritual defined Jewish practice, and all Jews (at least males) were required to attend the Temple at least once a year, on the Pilgrimage Festivals. Although there were smaller local altars and the beginnings of synagogue-like structures, it wasn't until after the destruction of the Temple that Jewish life became decentralized and the focus of ritual shifted from the altar to the home.

At that time, the synagogue became the center of public Jewish life, the home the private sphere. Both carried equal weight, for while synagogue rituals were critical, it was in the home that seders were celebrated, *b'rit milah* was observed, *tzedakah* was set aside, and children were educated in how to live a day-to-day Jewish life.

The synagogue took on three vital roles, which it retains today:

1. *Beit k'nesset,* "house of meeting": In the synagogue the important business of the community was carried out, not just its religious rituals. Announcements of communal issues would be made, leaders would address the community, and decisions affecting the entire community would be determined.
2. *Beit midrash,* "house of study": The synagogue gradually took on the role of educating children, but it also was central in the ongoing learning of the adults of the community. Daily *shiurim,* or classes, were attended by those able, and Shabbat learning was offered.
3. *Beit t'filah,* "house of prayer": The notion of communal prayer eventually developed from a systematic animal sacrifice presided over by priests to a systematic service presided over by learned laypeople and rabbis.

We know that women played no leadership roles in the ancient Temple or in the sacrificial system. Though women and men were both commanded to bring sacrifices, women could marry priests but could not function as priests themselves. We might have expected this to change under the decentralization of the second century, but in fact it did not. The Rabbis of the Talmud, fashioning the prayer book and the prayer service in the academies of the exile, did not reenvision a new role for women in the emerging synagogue structures, although there is archeological evidence to suggest that women held some positions of responsibility and leadership there.[1]

The synagogue as a house of prayer became a central motif throughout the ages. And the prayer book became the structure for defining how we pray, when we pray, and the words and methods of Jewish prayer. While there is some evidence of prayers written either by or for women, known in Yiddish as *techinas,* such *techinas* revolved around the three mitzvot that were central to women—

baking challah, lighting candles, and going to *mikveh*. The *techinas* expressed deep longing for health and prosperity, for children who would bring honor and husbands who would bring joy. Such expressions, while meaningful, beautiful, and historically significant, may not answer modern women's prayer needs.

Since the synagogue is so central to Jewish life today, it behooves us to revisit the question of women's leadership in our own congregations. Central to that issue is the question of the role of male leadership in the liberal synagogue. Years ago it was assumed that men would take on the leadership roles of rabbi, cantor, synagogue president, ritual chairman. Today that is no longer true, and more and more women take on those titles. Yet, at the same time, more and more congregants lament what has been called "the flight of men" from the synagogue. As women gain more public roles, more powerful titles, more leadership skills of both a religious and an administrative nature, functioning as rabbis, cantors, and synagogue lay leaders, fewer and fewer men take the challenge to do so themselves. Women flock to adult education classes in their synagogues; men now stay away. Are we seeing a "feminization" of the synagogue arena we have never seen before? Some claim men are abandoning the synagogue and leaving it solely to women. Others wonder if there is an implied threat to men and their masculinity when women take over leadership positions. Are we seeing a backlash on the part of men to the newly acquired public positions of women in their synagogues? Or are we seeing the devaluing of the synagogue by men once it becomes an egalitarian institution, and no longer an "old-boys network"?

THE TEXTS

1. Hannah's prayer, from I Samuel 2:1–10:

> Then Hannah prayed, saying:
>
> My heart exults in *Adonai*
> my strength is exalted by *Adonai*
> my mouth derides my foes
> as I rejoice in Your salvation.
>
> There is none holy as *Adonai,*
> For there is none beside You;
> There is no Rock like our God.
>
> Do not increase your high-flown speech,
> Let arrogance depart from your mouths!
> For *Adonai* is the God of knowledge,
> whose deeds are immeasurable.
>
> The warrior's bows are shattered,
> And the faltering are girded with strength.
> Those who were full sell themselves for bread,
> And those once hungry are full.
> While the barren woman bears seven children,
> The one with many children is bereaved.
>
> *Adonai* appoints life and death,
> Casts down to Sheol and lifts up.
> *Adonai* dispenses poverty or wealth,
> Casts down or lifts up,
>
> Lifting the poor from the dust,
> Raising the needy from the dunghill,
> Making them sit with nobles,
> Assigning them seats of honor.
> For the earth's pillars are *Adonai*'s,
> Who set the world upon them,
>
> Who guards the steps of the faithful
> While the wicked lie silent in darkness.

For not by might will a person prevail.

The foes of *Adonai* will be shattered,
As God thunders against them in the heavens,
Judging the ends of the earth,
Giving strength to God's king,
And raising the horn of victory for God's anointed.

2. Babylonian Talmud, *B'rachot* 31a:

Rav Hamnuna said: How many most important laws can be learned from these verses relating to Hannah! Now Hannah, she spoke in her heart: from this we learn that one who prays must direct his heart. Only her lips moved: from this we learn that he who prays must frame the words distinctly with his lips. But her voice could not be heard: from this, it is forbidden to raise one's voice in the *T'filah [Amidah]*. Therefore Eli thought she had been drunken: from this, that a drunken person is forbidden to say the *T'filah*. And Eli said unto her, How long wilt thou be drunken, etc. Rabbi Eleazar said: From this we learn that one who sees in his neighbor something unseemly must reprove him. And Hannah answered and said, No, my lord. 'Ulla, or as some say Rabbi Yosei bar Chanina, said: She said to him: Thou art no lord in this matter, nor does the holy spirit rest on thee, that thou suspectest me of this thing. Some say, She said to him: Thou art no lord, [meaning] the *Shechinah* and the holy spirit is not with you in that you take the harsher and not the more lenient view of my conduct. Dost thou not know that I am a woman of sorrowful spirit: I have drunk neither wine nor strong drink. Rabbi Eleazar said: From this we learn that one who is suspected wrongfully must clear himself. Count not thy handmaid for a daughter of Belial; a man who says the *T'filah* when drunk is like who serves idols. It is written here, Count not thy handmaid for a daughter of Belial, and it is written elsewhere, Certain sons of Belial have gone forth from the midst of thee. Just as there the term is used in connection with idolatry, so here. Then Eli answered and said, "Go in peace." Rabbi Eleazar said: From this we learn that one who suspects his neighbor of a fault that he has not committed must beg his pardon; nay more, he must bless him, as it says, And the God of Israel grant thy petition.

3. Babylonian Talmud, *B'rachot* 20b:

> Mishnah. Women, slaves, and minors are exempt from reciting the *Sh'ma* and from putting on *t'fillin*. But they are subject to the obligations of *t'filah* and mezuzah and Blessing after Meals.
>
> That they are exempt from the *Sh'ma* is self-evident—it is a positive precept for which there is a fixed time. . . . They are subject to the obligations of *t'filah*. Because this [is supplication for divine] mercy. . . .

4. Jeffrey K. Salkin, "Jewish Macho," *Reform Judaism* 26 (spring 1998): 28–30:

> Let's face it. The great unspoken crisis facing modern Judaism is the disengagement of men in large numbers. While no one mourns the exclusive male minyan, more and more men seem to be leaving the synagogue in the hands of women. . . . A major factor in male synagogue flight is careerism. As a predominantly upper middle class group, many Jewish men hold high power jobs that require long hours, commuting and business travel. Some of the most creative, assertive, and dynamic Jewish men simply don't have the time to bring these qualities to the synagogue community. . . . Another difficulty in exciting men about synagogue life is what we offer to get them there. Many congregations focus mainly on the education of children . . . if synagogues are child-centered, and if women are still primarily responsible for child-rearing, then the congregation becomes a place for women and children first. And finally, spirituality itself may have gotten a bad name. Men of all faiths often associate spirituality with so-called "feminine" characteristics: inwardness, openness, vulnerability and nurturing. By contrast, American masculinity connotes independence, industriousness, and competition.

5. Letters to the Editor, *Reform Judaism* 26 (summer 1998):

   a) Andy Curry:

   > Perhaps it is time to move toward a new (old) model: the synagogue as a "clearinghouse" for the fulfillment of obligations—mitzvot.

b) Rabbi Elyse Goldstein:

> Orthodox and Conservative synagogues, which remain bastions of male privilege and male power, have a clear "in-group" whose members retain a solid showing. Those synagogue which preach, teach and practice sharing of power, entitlement of women, and even experimentation with feminist forms have no clear "in-group" and much less prestige for men *just for being men.* It is historically true that all institutions which were once closed systems of male advantage and are now open to women are subsequently devalued by men. If men among men do not openly discuss the convergence of egalitarianism and male flight, we will not get to the deeper, though more complicated, level of this issue.

THE QUESTIONS

1. Women are clearly obligated to pray. How can we understand this in a liberal context, in which Jews may or may not fulfill the mitzvah of public prayer (i.e., *Shacharit, Minchah,* and *Maariv*) services daily? Might women fulfill prayer obligations differently? Think about what the notion of "obligations in prayer" might mean in a non-halachic movement.

2. Do you think men and women pray differently? If not, should they be equally obligated? If so, should they have different obligations? Different prayers or prayer books? How might the prayers of women differ from those of men? Do you think a prayer book written entirely by women would be different from the prayer book we have now?

3. The introductory question of *equalization* and *specialization* is important in the discussion of women and the synagogue. Do we want women to join the ranks of committed synagogue Jews simply as Jews, that is, equal access without any issue of gender coming into play, or do we want them to have a specific—and perhaps unique or different—role in the synagogue as women?

4. What role do women play in your house of meeting, house of study, house of prayer? Do they hold positions of communal leadership? Do they teach? Do they participate actively in service leadership, *aliyot* to the Torah, reading from Torah, and the like? If so, does their participation "feel" different from that of men? Ask a woman who is a leader to describe her role. Then ask a man. Are their perceptions different?

5. Do you feel that the synagogue is being "feminized" by the amount of attention paid to women's issues, women rabbis, and the like? Do you think more women than men are attracted to the synagogue? If so, why? Do you think there is a backlash against the rise of women in synagogue leadership and synagogue programming on women's spirituality? What do you think is the cause of this? And what should synagogues do about this?

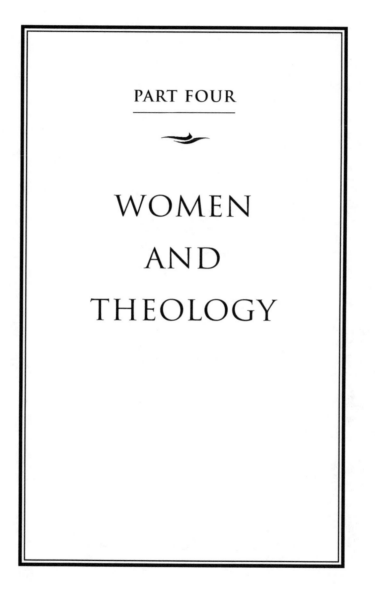

PART FOUR

WOMEN
AND
THEOLOGY

10

⁓

God Language and Theological Issues

THE ISSUES

When it comes to expressing our relationship to God, we are limited in that we have only human language, only words. Thus this indescribable, irrational system of belief must somehow be expressed through rational phrases and descriptions, and that may frustrate us. We get trapped in the one-dimensionality of the prayer book and in the anthropomorphism of the Torah, in God's "hands" and "ears"and "heart." As best we can, we ought to be thinking about these aspects of God as the tradition does when encountering human descriptions of Divinity. To avoid this problem, we are taught to add the phrase *k'ilu* or *kivyachol,* "as it were" or "as if," when assigning human characteristics or feelings to God.

So how then can we talk about God? Does the language of a relationship have some effect on the relationship itself? In other words, does what we say color what we believe, or does what we believe color what we say, or both?

As children, we are taught about God through stories, and we come to know God as a King, a Father, an all-powerful and mighty Being. But as we grow into adulthood and redefine our beliefs in a more sophisticated way, we often find ourselves uncomfortable with those simplistic childhood images. Our spiritual experience and our spiritual "vocabulary" have increased and broadened, but our prayer language has not.

Male imagery of God continues to shape the way we think about God, Judaism, and the role of men and women altogether in Jewish religious life. Some have suggested that God language is not a matter of semantics but theology, for God language will ultimately not only reflect our beliefs but also cast them, change them, or create them. Language can be poetic, esoteric, or symbolic in nature, but it is never arbitrary; language both *describes* and *creates* reality. While people rightly protest that symbols are not reality but only symbols, through centuries of familiarity symbols lose their transparency and come to be seen as descriptive of, and not merely as metaphors for, reality. If God is Father, and the Children of Israel are His "firstborn sons," then women are perpetually a second class, adjuncts, the wives and mothers of those fathers and sons.

The representation of God in the Torah is predominantly male, expressed not only through the male pronoun, but through many male characteristics, such as God as a "Man of war" (Exodus 15:3). Judith Plaskow writes, "God's maleness is so deeply and firmly established as part of the Jewish conception of God that it is almost difficult to document. It is simply part of the lenses through which God is seen. Maleness is not a distinct attribute, separable from God's anger or mercy or justice. Rather, it is expressed through the total picture of God in Jewish texts and liturgy."[1] Jewish philosophers such as Maimonides taught an absolute invisible, incorporeal God and rejected the anthropomorphism of the Torah as a projection of human need, noting that "the Torah speaks in a human language." In other words, we are stuck with human language, so by necessity that language will be limited, and any attempt to see the language as anything other than symbolic is futile.

But intertwined into that human, male symbolism are issues of male dominance and male authority. If God is Father and King, Warrior and "Lord of hosts," and if our Jewish task is to be godlike, then how can women ever be godlike? It is no accident that women do not experience themselves as equals within a society that encourages a masculine image for its highest Divinity. And it is no accident that the highest source of our values, the ultimate model of holiness, the pinnacle of our search for meaning, is imagined in such male terms.

In traditional Judaism, God's relationship to us is based on hierarchical opposites: Father/son; King/servant. God is majestic, distant, exalted. This God is a Being utterly outside of us, above, insisting on obedience and authority, punishing the wicked and rewarding the faithful. Seen within this context, human male dominance makes sense and is supported by the theological system as well as the legal system.

Language that envisions God as male, or female, correlates to the emergence of gender as a defining concern. What we say about God colors what we say about ourselves on a personal level. On a communal level, a religious society uses its theology to justify what women can/cannot and should/should not do within its social system. Thus God's maleness, a male priesthood, and the chosenness of "first-born sons" all connect to a preoccupation with the rules, roles, and rights of women.

What we say about God becomes not a matter of semantics, but a matter of faith, a reflection of our beliefs, and an integral part of our received tradition.

THE TEXTS

1. Rita Gross, "Female God Language in a Jewish Context," in *Womanspirit Rising: A Feminist Reader in Religion,* ed. Carol Christ and Judith Plaskow (New York: Harper and Row, 1979), 170:

   > A God language does not really tell us about God, but it does tell us a considerable amount about those who use the God language.

2. Judith Plaskow, *Standing Again at Sinai: Judaism from a Feminist Perspective* (San Francisco: Harper and Row, 1990), 183:

   > Were feminist objections to Jewish God-language confined to the issues of gender, the manipulation of pronouns and creation of female imagery would fairly easily resolve the difficulties described . . . while feminist criticisms of traditional language begin with gender, they come to focus on the deeper issue of images of God's power as dominance.

3. Annette Daum, "Language and Liturgy," in *Daughters of the King: Women and the Synagogue,* ed. Susan Grossman and Rivka Haut (Philadelphia: Jewish Publication Society, 1992), 187:

   > Until now, the prayer book has expressed the spiritual yearnings of half the Jewish People, the men who were the writers, editors, and translators of a liturgy that was designed for use by men. Still, many of the prayers reflect human experience such as prayers for health, wisdom, forgiveness, and justice, as well as praise and thanksgiving. Feminine imagery appears, for example, in the Hallel, which speaks of barren women becoming mothers. It is difficult to determine whether the prayer reflects female yearnings or male priorities—the desire for progeny—which women internalize.
   >
   > No matter how sensitive, these prayers, written from a male perspective, assume that women's only priority is to fulfill her biological function—to bear children. Theses prayers are highly selective, reflecting a Biblical perspective (male) that features the Matriarchs as revered female role models. The editors of our prayer books traditionally excluded prayers by other biblical

women, such as Miriam and Deborah, which offer alternative role models.

4. On the very last page of the Reform High Holy Day *machzor* (*Gates of Repentance: The New Union Prayerbook for the Days of Awe,* ed. Chaim Stern [New York: Central Conference of American Rabbis, 1996], 549–50), this alternative or addition to the traditional *Avinu Malkeinu,* "Our Father, Our King" prayer appears:

Shechinah, M'Kor Chayeinu

Shechinah, Source of our lives, hear our plea—spare us, have compassion upon us.

Motherly Presence, Source of our lives, keep us in your care, for we are your sons and your daughters.

Holy Presence, Source of our lives, teach us to know our limits.

Gentle Presence, Source of our lives, guide us in pleasant ways.

Guiding Presence, Source of our lives, teach us mercy and justice.

Nurturing Presence, Source of our lives, support those who struggle for peace and justice.

Compassionate Presence, Source of our lives, turn our lamentation to exultation and our sorrow to joy.

Caring Presence, Source of our lives, bless our land and all the work of our hands.

Loving Presence, Source of our lives, assemble your people from the four corners of the world in their land.

Shechinah, Source of our lives, build peace in Jerusalem, our holy city.

THE QUESTIONS

1. Discuss Rita Gross's point that God language tells us more about ourselves than about God. How is this manifest in our prayer book? In our speech about God? What do we say about ourselves when we pray?

2. On Judith Plaskow's point: Think about any time you have heard a speaker use a female pronoun for God. Did it result in snickers or laughter by the audience and comments on that choice of pronoun even if the speaker was never speaking about women or feminism at all? Why? Could the discomfort with female pronouns for God point to a deeper ambivalence with female power, authority, and responsibility altogether? Or is it just discomfort with the unfamiliar?

3. Discuss Daum's thesis that the prayer book, no matter how sensitive, still reflects a male perspective. Does the addition of the Matriarchs change that assumption? Would the addition of prayers especially about women's lives (e.g., first menstruation) make it worse or better? What would prayers using "alternative role models" like Deborah and Miriam be?

4. What words would you choose to use to describe God? Write a list of adjectives and see how they might fit into your prayer life.

5. How does the *Shechinah, M'Kor Chayeinu* prayer make you feel? Would it stir you the same, more, or less than "Our Father, Our King"? Can you imagine reciting it in your congregation? Why or why not? At each service or at a special service? Just once or at all the services? Would you miss the traditional *Avinu Malkeinu*? Why or why not?

11

The *Shechinah*

THE ISSUES

In an attempt to speak about God in more encompassing terms, many people wonder if the tradition can offer us feminine imagery and feminine terms for God while still remaining within a strictly monotheistic framework.

One way to do so is by reappropriating the "goddess" aspects of *Adonai.* Surely our ancestors saw in the One God all the various aspects of their old gods and goddesses: power, truth, compassion, justice, strength, wisdom. Instead of separate gods and goddesses having only one of each characteristic, they felt that the One God had them all. When they replaced the many with The One, they must have desired to incorporate both the aspects of the gods and the aspects of the goddesses in *Adonai,* who was the One God replacing their old pantheon.

Some feel this methodology enables the tradition to speak to women who perceive that Judaism has not offered them a spirituality or a voice. Rabbi Lynn Gottlieb calls this restoring the " . . . pre-biblical archetype of a female Creatrix to contemporary Jewish liturgy."[1] Furthermore, she suggests that what we perceive as "traditional" Jewish symbols can be recast into their more ancient prototype, linking them specifically with a female aspect of the godhead. She writes, "The use of candles, braided bread, and the liturgical image of the Sabbath Queen and Bride link Jewish women on an intuitive, if not explicit, level to the feminine divine."[2]

Some feel we should push even further and now use for God the very word "goddess," without fears of being branded as "pagan." Supporters of this idea question whether the word "goddess" has any more pagan or polytheistic association than the word "god." They argue, doesn't the word "god" conjure up the old gods just as "goddess" conjures up the old goddesses? Why should the word "goddess" be any more pagan than the word "god"? Advocates of this methodology argue that the charge of paganism has no real basis and is used only to squelch any discussion of female God language, for the fear of returning to this unknown, unexplored territory of paganism. Advocates of using the word "goddess" assert that the fear of paganism in our postmodern world is simply groundless.

Others suggest that we turn to the tradition for feminine images but not feminine terminology. Adding the Matriarchs and finding places in the Bible or midrash where God is imagined as a mother, or in other feminine ways, would adjust the abundance of words like "Father" and "King." For example, God is called the Rock who gives birth (Deuteronomy 32), and in the same chapter the Rock is portrayed as an object of suckling. The prophet Isaiah speaks of God as a mother (Isaiah 42, 49, and 66). Job speaks of God's womb (Job 38). These kind of images could be rediscovered and inserted into our existing prayer book.

A third possibility is to add the use of *Shechinah* to our repertoire of terminologies for God. Jewish feminists have "rediscovered" the concept of *Shechinah*. The Hebrew name *Shechinah* literally means "dwelling" and appears as a name for God's presence in rabbinic literature of the second century C.E. The midrash speaks of God placing "His *Shechinah*" in the midst of Israel and of the *Shechinah* resting upon individuals when they study Torah. The *Shechinah* is pictured as going into exile along with the Jewish people, and thus she reflects the state of the entire Jewish people on a metaphoric level. Depicted often as luminous light, the *Shechinah* shines with God's radiance. It is a manifestation of divinity that indicates God's presence at a given place. The later medieval Jewish philosophers described the *Shechinah* as a separate entity itself, created by God. According to Y'hudah HaLevi, the *Shechinah* dwelt first in the desert Tabernacle, then in the Temple; but when the Temple was destroyed, the *Shechinah* ceased to appear and will only reappear with the coming of the Messiah.[3]

It is only with the development of Kabbalah, Jewish mysticism, however, that the *Shechinah* takes on feminine characteristics. In the late twelfth and thirteenth centuries C.E., the *Shechinah* begins to be described as princess, daughter, and the feminine principle in the world.

However, *Shechinah* offers no complete answers, and she is not a panacea. She is a projection of what male mystics believed femininity and the feminine principle in the world to be: passive and receptive. According to Kabbalah, she occupies the lowest rung, the tenth and last of the *s'firot,* or divine emanations, that created the world. As such, she dwells the closest to earth and closest to the "dark" powers. As a passive "vessel," she has no light of her own and receives the divine light from the other *s'firot.* Because the *Shechinah* contains so many facets of stereotypical female passivity, we will have to separate the traditional kabbalistic *Shechinah* from the *Shechinah* we need and crave; though on a metaphoric level, *Shechinah* holds tremendous power for us. The angels are her servants. She is the divine principle of the people Israel. She, together with Israel symbolizing the "wife" and God the "husband," replaces the goddess and yet remains part of the monotheistic vision of the One God. The *Shechinah* is the closest first contact in the mystical struggle for communion with God. If, as according to the kabbalists, the mitzvot (commandments) act as vehicles to reunite the masculine principle with the feminine, and as an attempt to reharmonize God and the *Shechinah,* who originally were One; and if Torah study and prayer bring a person into direct contact with her and thus with God, then the ultimate goal of Judaism is one of harmony. We must look for harmony between God and *Shechinah,* between masculine and feminine, and ultimately between male and female persons. As the *Shechinah* and God are One, so too the masculine and feminine ultimately are also one and need only be brought back together. We do so through daily acts that reunite the broken fragments of masculinity and femininity.

THE TEXTS

1. Tikva Frymer-Kensky, *In The Wake of the Goddesses* (New York: The Free Press, 1992), 183:

   Throughout the history of Western religion, the many facets of mother, of the wife-of-god image and the Indweller of Zion result in new powerful female images. The post-Biblical legendary writings (the Midrashim) continue the picture of Mother Rachel as the great intercessor.... Mothers in heaven, they weep and pray for their children.... The Sabbath became the queen who married God and Israel. The Shechinah ("the indweller") became the symbol of Divine immanence, residing in Jerusalem, among the people, and in humanity.... These mediating figures did not disappear because they addressed the great existential dilemma of monotheism, the centrality of humankind, and its sense of inadequacy in the face of divine power.... These female images are not necessarily bad for women. Having a literary figure of Woman-Wisdom can reinforce the idea that women are wise; having a beloved Zion teaches that women are lovable. Similarly, the later Jewish images of the sabbath Queen-Bride and the Torah are positive female images that can raise women's prestige and reinforce women's self-esteem.

2. Moses Cordovero, *The Palm Tree of Deborah,* trans. Louis Jacobs (New York: Sepher-Hermon Press, 1960), chapter 9:

   A man must be careful to behave so that the Shechinah cleaves always to him and never departs. Now, it is obvious that the Shechinah cannot be with a bachelor for the Shechinah is mainly from the female. Man stands between the two females, the physical female below who receives food, clothing and conjugal rights from him, and the Shechinah who stands above him to bless him with these, which he, in turn, gives to the wife of his covenant.... Now a man separates himself from his wife at times for one of three reasons: 1) when she is in her period of separation; 2) when he studies Torah and lives apart from her; 3) when he journeys from home and keeps himself from sin. During these times the Shechinah cleaves to him and does not leave him, so that he not be forsaken and separate but always the perfect man, male and female....

3. From the Bible:
   a) Deuteronomy 32:13: "God suckled us with honey from the rock. . . ."
   b) Deuteronomy 32:18: "The Rock that had hardly just borne you. . . ."
   c) Isaiah 66:13: "As a mother comforts her child, so I will comfort you. . . ."
   d) Isaiah 42:14: "I cry out like a woman in labor, I pant and I gasp. . . ."
   e) Isaiah 49:15: "Can a mother forget her babe, or stop loving the child of her womb? Even these could forget, but I could not forget you!"
   f) Psalm 22:11: "Since the womb, you have been my mother, my God. . . ."
   g) Job 38:29: "Out of whose womb came the ice. . .?"

THE QUESTIONS

1. Discuss Frymer-Kensky's quote. What positive role can reinforcing God as Mother play in our modern world? Does the strength of a Mary figure in Christianity point to a basic human need? How can Judaism answer that need?

2. Discuss the Cordovero quote on the *Shechinah*. How is the "perfect man" both male and female? The kabbalistic notion is that what we do on earth mirrors what happens above. How do you feel about the notion of a "female" above who delivers blessings on the husband to give to his wife below? What are those blessings, and how do they mirror what goes on in heaven?

3. Have you ever been to a service where female pronouns were used for God? How did it feel to you? Should we use female pronouns or female imagery "just to make a point"? Why or why not?

4. How do you feel about using the term "goddess"? *Shechinah?* God as Mother?

5. How do you feel about the "mother" imagery of the biblical texts? Would you substitute these terms into our prayer book for the terms we have now, add them, interchange them, use them in a whole service or part of a service? How do you imagine the congregation would react? How would you answer the critics?

12

~

The Question of Changing Liturgy

THE ISSUES

Let us say that a congregation has decided to change its liturgy from an exclusively male language. Where would it start? What would be the larger issues than which particular word to use? And which words *would* the congregation use?

First, we have to agree that language is not arbitrary. When we say "table," we mean table, not chair. "Animal" is the generic term for certain creatures, but "cow" is specific. No one would argue that "cow" can also mean "chicken." Yet some still argue that "he" can also mean "she." "God" is generic for that Being we try to describe, but "He" and "King" and "Father" are not generic.

There are several ways to approach this new area of God talk in an attempt to move away from a mostly male religious lexicon. Since English is a nongendered language, we could start there. We can simply use neutral terms for God—substitute "Ruler" for "King," "Parent" for "Father." We can speak of God as "God" instead of either "He" or "She." But such neutralization works only when the listeners divest themselves of all male stereotypes and archetypes, so that the word "parent" does not automatically conjure up a father, either heavenly or human. This is difficult because of centuries of saturation of male imagery and the use of the word "Father." This neutral terminology works best with young children, not yet overly familiar with male archetypes. Some say, though, that neutral terminology does not correct the male imagery; it simply neutralizes it. That is, when we say "God," we no longer hear how male the language has been in the past, nor are we aware of how many centuries we have been saying "He." Others worry that though we *say* "God," we still *mean* "He." Neutralizing the words does not always neutralize the effect of centuries of predominant images. And neutral language has limitations, because we learn that we are created in God's image, and we ourselves are gendered beings. By degendering God, we minimize our own human gender. For some, that is liberating; for others, threatening. Thus neutralization, for some, is an excellent first step, while for others, it is the final and most egalitarian step.

Another approach is to change the language to include "She." The use of "She," proponents say, helps point out the "he-ness" of "He." If we never really meant that God was a "He," we should have no problem whatsoever using the term "She."

The real challenge, of course, is Hebrew. Like changing "He" to "She" in English, we can do the same in Hebrew. We can change the masculine gendered Hebrew of *baruch atah* to the feminine form of *b'ruchah at.* We can switch back and forth. Or we can wait and pray that linguists will soon develop a nongendered form in the Hebrew language! Marcia Falk has done groundbreaking work in her *Book of Blessings,* offering a new Hebrew that speaks not only in a nongendered way, but also in a nonhierarchical way. She suggests a new formula of "We bless the Source of Life" (in Hebrew: *n'vareich et m'kor hachayim*) to replace *baruch atah.* The word "we" in Hebrew takes neither the male nor female form, so it is a truly "neutral" pronoun. Rather than God remaining the distant King, or becoming a Queen, God becomes the Core of Life, the Fountain of Life, and other more imminent (inner) rather than transcendent (outer) idioms. Her use of language moves the enterprise not only away from gender but also away from traditional formulations of God as over us, reigning supreme, and demanding our praise.[1] Critics say that this "humanizes" God and brings Divinity down to a very earthly level. What about those people who do believe in a transcendent

God, wholly outside and above us? And we will still need to teach that *melech* means "king" in Hebrew, because we want our children to learn Hebrew properly. But we can teach them the art of translation and of using many words to translate one idea.

THE TEXTS

1. The paragraph of the *V'ahavta* prayer in the *siddur* that begins "You shall love *Adonai* your God . . ." comes from the Torah, in the Book of Deuteronomy, chapter 6. In the Hebrew, it is rendered in the male singular throughout, relating directly to the individual male worshiper. Alongside the traditional form provided below is another form that uses the feminine singular throughout:

הֲרֵי אַתָּה מְקֻדָּשׁ לִי בְּטַבַּעַת זוֹ כְּדַת מֹשֶׁה וְיִשְׂרָאֵל.

traditional

וְאָהַבְתָּ אֵת יְיָ אֱלֹהֶיךָ, בְּכָל-לְבָבְךָ, וּבְכָל-נַפְשְׁךָ, וּבְכָל-מְאֹדֶךָ. וְהָיוּ
הַדְּבָרִים הָאֵלֶּה, אֲשֶׁר אָנֹכִי מְצַוְּךָ הַיּוֹם,
עַל-לְבָבֶךָ: וְשִׁנַּנְתָּם לְבָנֶיךָ, וְדִבַּרְתָּ בָּם בְּשִׁבְתְּךָ בְּבֵיתֶךָ, וּבְלֶכְתְּךָ
בַדֶּרֶךְ וּבְשָׁכְבְּךָ, וּבְקוּמֶךָ. וּקְשַׁרְתָּם לְאוֹת
עַל-יָדֶךָ, וְהָיוּ לְטֹטָפֹת בֵּין עֵינֶיךָ, וּכְתַבְתָּם עַל מְזֻזֹת בֵּיתֶךָ
וּבִשְׁעָרֶיךָ:

לְמַעַן תִּזְכְּרוּ וַעֲשִׂיתֶם אֶת-כָּל-מִצְוֹתָי, וִהְיִיתֶם קְדשִׁים לֵאלֹהֵיכֶם:
אֲנִי יְיָ אֱלֹהֵיכֶם, אֲשֶׁר הוֹצֵאתִי אֶתְכֶם מֵאֶרֶץ
מִצְרַיִם, לִהְיוֹת לָכֶם לֵאלֹהִים, אֲנִי יְיָ אֱלֹהֵיכֶם:

feminine

וְאָהַבְתְּ אֵת יְיָ אֱלֹהָיִךְ, בְּכָל-לְבָבֵךְ, וּבְכָל-נַפְשֵׁךְ, וּבְכָל-מְאֹדֵךְ. וְהָיוּ
הַדְּבָרִים הָאֵלֶּה, אֲשֶׁר אָנֹכִי מְצַוָּךְ הַיּוֹם,
עַל-לְבָבֵךְ: וְשִׁנַּנְתָּם לִבְנוֹתַיִךְ, וְדִבַּרְתְּ בָּם בְּשִׁבְתֵּךְ בְּבֵיתֵךְ,
וּבְלֶכְתֵּךְ בַדֶּרֶךְ וּבְשָׁכְבֵּךְ, וּבְקוּמֵךְ. וּקְשַׁרְתִּים לְאוֹת
עַל-יָדֵךְ, וְהָיוּ לְטֹטָפֹת בֵּין עֵינַי, וּכְתַבְתִּים עַל מְזֻזֹת
בֵּיתֵךְ וּבִשְׁעָרָיִךְ:

לְמַעַן תִּזְכֹּרְנָה וַעֲשִׂיתֶן אֶת-כָּל-מִצְוֹתַי, וִהְיִיתֶן קְדשׁוֹת לֵאלֹהֵיכֶן:
אֲנִי יְיָ אֱלֹהֵיכֶן, אֲשֶׁר הוֹצֵאתִי אֶתְכֶן מֵאֶרֶץ
מִצְרַיִם, לִהְיוֹת לָךְ לֵאלֹהִים, אֲנִי יְיָ אֱלֹהֵיכֶן:

V'ahavt eit Adonai Elohayich b'chol l'vaveich uv'chol nafsheich uv'-chol m'odeich. V'hayu hadvarim ha-eileh asher anochi m'tzaveich hayom al l'vaveich. V'shinantam livnotayich v'dibart bam b'shivteich b'veiteich uv'lechteich baderech uv'shochbeich uv'kumeich. Uk'shartim l'ot al yadeich v'hayu l'totafot bein einayich uch'tavtim al m'zuzot beit-eich uvisharayich.

L'maan tizkornah vaasiten et kol mitzvotai vih'yiten k'doshot leilohe-ichen. Ani Aodnai Eloheichen asher hotzeiti etchen mei-eretz Mitzrayim lih'yot lachen leilohim ani Adonai Eloheichen.

2. Dr. Joseph H. Hertz (the late chief rabbi of the British Empire), introduction to *The Authorised Daily Prayer Book* (New York: Bloch Publishing, 1974):

   The Jewish Prayer Book, or Siddur, is of paramount importance in the life of the Jewish people. To Israel's faithful hosts in the past, as to its loyal sons and daughters in the present, the Siddur has been the gate to communion with their Father in Heaven; and at the same time, it has been a mighty spiritual bond that united them to their scattered brethren the world over. No other book in the whole range of Jewish literature that stretches over three millennia and more, comes so close to the life of the Jewish masses as does the Prayer Book. The Siddur is a daily companion, and the whole drama of earthly existence—its joys and sorrows; workdays, Sabbaths and historic and Solemn Festivals; birth, marriage and death—is sanctified by the formulae of devotion in that holy book. To millions of Jews, every word of it is familiar and loved, and its phrases and Responses, especially in the sacred melodies associated with them, can stir them to the depths of their being. . . .

3. Here are three nongendered translations of the *Kiddush,* found in Anita Diamant, *The New Jewish Wedding Book* (New York: Simon and Schuster, 1993), 186–87:

   a) Joan Kaye: "Holy One of Blessing, your blessing fills creation, forming the fruit of the vine."

   b) Rabbi Danny Siegal: "We acknowledge the Unity of all within the sovereignty of God, expressing our appreciation for this wine, symbol and aid of our rejoicing."

   c) Rabbi Burt Jacobson: "Be blessed, O Infinite God, the Power and Majesty of all, creating the fruit of the vine."

THE QUESTIONS

1. Read the *V'ahavt* out loud, either individually or as a group. How does it feel? Would you feel comfortable using this in a service? Would men read the traditional version and women the other— or could everyone read the *V'ahavt*?

2. Discuss Hertz's comments on the power of the *siddur*. Indeed, the *siddur* does bind us to each other across time and space. The *Sh'ma* is the same wherever you go. How can we balance the need for that bond with the need for change?

3. How much are we willing to change the Hebrew when it comes from the Torah? How do you feel about changing the language of the Torah itself in the *V'ahavta*? This leads to a larger question for each of us: What is our relationship with Torah? What is its source of sacredness for us? Are its words just words or messages from the Divine? What does changing those words mean for us?

4. How do you feel about the nongendered translations like the *Kiddush*? How are they different from each other, and does each one give you a different "message" about God? What do we lose when we let go of "Lord our God" and "King of the universe?" What do we gain? Do the gains and losses balance, in your opinion?

5. Does God language matter to you? Why or why not? Have your opinions on this changed over the years? How does your congregation deal with God language?

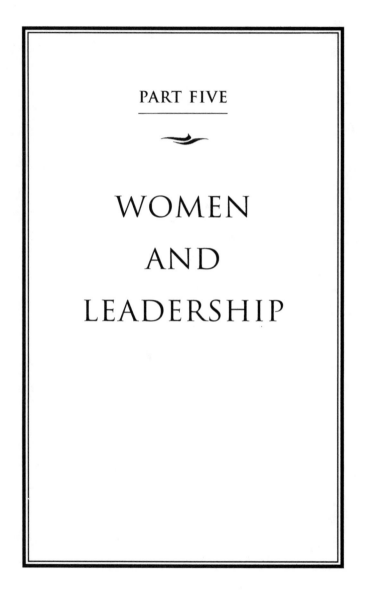

PART FIVE

WOMEN
AND
LEADERSHIP

13

A Brief History of
Women in the Rabbinate

The first woman rabbi, ordained June 3, 1972 by the Reform Movement, was truly a "first" in history. But while it is true that Sally Priesand's ordination shook the foundations of the Jewish world and changed all previous facts and figures relating to the rabbinate, she was not the first woman who had desired or tried to become a rabbi. Others before her had yearned and felt called to the rabbinate. Rabbi Priesand's ordination did not occur in a vacuum, for it was not until then that the time was ripe for the ordination of women.

Priesand entered Hebrew Union College–Jewish Institute of Religion, the Reform seminary, during the women's-lib era of the 1960s. She freely admits that her motive was never to "rock the boat," but simply to become a rabbi. It was her good luck that at that particular moment in history the college had decided it was time to keep up with the new demands of women and the advancements for women in the secular world.

Since the early nineteenth century, Reform Judaism had, at least on paper, ensured the religious equality of women. Confirmation replaced bar mitzvah as an all-male rite of passage, giving equal access to the religious strivings to both teenage boys and girls. As early as 1851, Isaac Mayer Wise had removed separate seating from his synagogue, Anshe Emeth in Albany, New York. But men still made the rules, and so men could bend them, or even break them, to "allow" women's entrance into such male bastions as *aliyot* to the Torah. It was not until the 1920s that the question was raised of whether opportunities for equal religious expression might also include entrance for women into the upper echelons of religious decision making, that is, into the rabbinate.

As early as 1919 a woman named Martha Neumark had begun to study at the Reform rabbinical seminary. In 1921 she was allowed to lead a High Holy Day congregation, marking her entrance into the public rabbinic arena. It was that move that prompted the president of the seminary at that time, Kaufmann Kohler, to form a faculty committee to study the feasibility of ordaining women. This debate around women's ordination emerged officially in 1922, at a conference of the faculty of Hebrew Union College. The debating parties questioned whether Jewish law might permit women's ordination. They wondered whether women could maintain their devotion to home and family given the time-consuming responsibilities of the rabbinate. The rabbis also worried whether ordaining women would create an irreparable schism within the larger Jewish community. Despite their concerns, however, the faculty of the seminary voted in favor of women's ordination. A few months later, the lay board of governors, upon whom the final decision rested, rejected the vote and restricted ordination from the college to men only. Though women attended the seminary as students from as early as 1900, they were not to be ordained until 1972.

Strangely enough, it was in Nazi Germany that the first woman actually held a position with a rabbinic title. Regina Jonas, a student at the liberal seminary in Berlin, was empowered in 1935 with a special diploma to "hold rabbinic office." She ministered to the Jews in the Terezin concentration camp and died in Auschwitz in 1944.

Everyone must have anticipated that there would be a ripple effect following Priesand's ordination, and indeed there was. The Reconstructionist Movement ordained Sandy Eisenberg Sasso in 1974, and the Conservative Movement ordained Amy Eilberg in 1983.

This ripple effect continues today. While the Orthodox Movement still does not ordain women, it has begun to deal with the demands of its own female leadership. A yearly Orthodox feminist conference in New York attracts thousands of participants. In 1998 Lincoln Square Synagogue, a modern Orthodox synagogue in New York, hired Julie Joseph as "congregational intern" in a para-rabbinic position to offer counseling, classes, and other professional services, though her responsibilities did not include preaching or other worship tasks. Other Orthodox communities have followed suit, and today there is an official position of *yoetzet halachah,* female halachic advisor, in several traditional communities.

Many people believe that the ordination of women has completely changed the face of organized Jewish life. Female rabbis often bring feminist concerns into their work, along with a sense of collective responsibility as women. Female rabbis are acutely aware that people notice their gender and pay special attention, often comparing them to other female rabbis they have heard or seen. Female rabbis may also feel that they represent *all* women when they are on the *bimah.* What were once considered solely women's issues, belonging to the Sisterhood or women's auxiliaries, are now discussed from the *bimah* and at conferences of major mainstream Jewish organizations. In sermons and study groups, the female characters of the Bible are studied, examined, and dissected as never before. The issues of sexual harassment and power hierarchies in organized Jewish life have come to the forefront. Gender stereotyping in textbooks is being analyzed and corrected. All this might have come about anyway, with the advances of feminism into Judaism. But there is no doubt that the presence of women in positions of religious and communal authority, influence, and decision making has pushed what have been previously identified as "marginal" issues into the consciousness of the mainstream.

Most of the women in the rabbinate today would agree that they are perceived differently from their male colleagues. Put simply, people experience female rabbis differently than they experience male ones. And they experience Judaism, the gender issues of the prayer book, and the whole question of the male imagery of God differently with a woman rabbi. The very notion of a woman rabbi challenges us to recognize that for centuries we thought male rabbis were the norm. By hearing the same stories retold now by women, by being at the same events now led by women, by simply sitting in the pews and looking up to see women in front, many Jews say they have come to see their total Jewish experience differently.

THE TEXTS

1. Traditional texts on women's communal leadership:
   a) *Sifrei* on Deuteronomy 17:15: "You shall be free to set a king over yourself: a king, but not a queen."
   b) Maimonides, "Laws of Kings" 1:5: "Only men may be appointed [to positions of authority] in Israel."
   c) Talmud, *Bava Kama* 15a, *Tosafot:* "If the people accept a woman as a judge, as was the case with D'vorah, then she is permitted to fill that function."

2. Robert Gordis, "The Ordination of Women," in *The Ordination of Women as Rabbis,* ed. Simon Greenberg (New York: Jewish Theological Seminary of America, 1988), 48, 64:

   . . . Rabbis today bear the oldest honorific designation in continuous use in human history. The title "rabbi" is far older than any honorary degree or academic distinction in vogue today. At the same time, the rabbinate represents virtually a new calling, since the functions designated by this ancient title have undergone a far-reaching transformation. . . . Advocates of the ordination of women are not asking that women act like men, only that they act like rabbis. There is nothing specifically masculine involved in teaching, preaching, counseling, or engaging in any other aspects of the rabbinate. . . .

3. Here are some quotes from women rabbis on their being female and a rabbi, from "Tosefta: Additional Voice," in "Wisdom You Are My Sister: 25 Years of Women in the Rabbinate," ed. Donna Berman, *CCAR Journal: A Reform Jewish Quarterly* 44 (summer 1997):
   a) Rabbi Karen Bookman Kaplan: "I believe some congregations select a female rabbi assuming she will be more easily controlled and dictated to by the board."
   b) Rabbi Beth Davidson: "I have been able to be a rabbi who happens to be a woman, not a woman who happens to be a rabbi, and that is a blessing. . . ."
   c) Rabbi Elka Abrahamson: "We as women can play a role in imitating the Divine through bold efforts to breathe a new

neshama into worship. . . ."

d) Rabbi Camille Shira Angel: "If we accept egalitarianism as
   our final stopping place, we Reformers leave intact the
   structures, texts, history, liturgy and images that testify
   against us and exclude half of us. We need to go beyond
   merely 'adding' women to a tradition that remains basical-
   ly unaltered, by creating a Judaism that all of us have a role
   in shaping."

THE QUESTIONS

1. Do you believe female rabbis are perceived differently than male rabbis? If so, in what ways? Can you give specific examples of those differences? What do you think accounts for these differences?

2. From your experience, do you believe female rabbis behave or act differently than male rabbis in the same situations (e.g., a funeral, counseling, preaching)? How would you describe the difference?

3. Do you agree with Robert Gordis that "there is nothing specifically masculine involved in teaching, preaching, counseling, or engaging in any other aspects of the rabbinate"? Has the rabbinate "taken on" any masculine characteristics as a result of being only men for so many generations? What about the "paternal" nature of the rabbi?

4. What is your reaction to the various statements of the female rabbis in the third set of texts? Do you think egalitarianism should be our final stop? Do you agree with Rabbi Kaplan that "some congregations select a female rabbi assuming she will be more easily controlled and dictated to by the board"? How do you feel about women rabbis being the pioneers of new kinds of worship? Do you think a rabbi's identity should be linked to gender?

5. Imagine that, for all of Jewish history until the present, only women had been allowed to become rabbis. In your lifetime, men had become rabbis for the first time. What would be your reaction? Your concerns? Fears? Anticipations? Expectations?

14

~

Where Do We Go from Here?
Men, Sexuality, and Integration

THE ISSUES

So much has changed for women in the Jewish world over the last decades that it is tempting to say the "woman's question" is over. Women are rabbis in the Reform, Conservative, and Reconstructionist denominations and present in the leadership of Orthodoxy. Women serve as congregational presidents and as directors of national organizations. Jewish education for girls is practically a universal given now in the entire Jewish world. So where do we go from here?

Three areas remain critical challenges for the new generation of female Jewish leadership. One is the challenge of male reaction and male inclusion into the growing network of "women's spirituality" and the advances of women into Jewish life. The second is the area of Judaism and sexuality and, with the increasing visibility of gays and lesbians in the Jewish world, a growing awareness of their spiritual needs and particular experiences of exclusion and inclusion, as well. And the third is the ultimate task of integrating our female selves with our Jewish selves.

Jewish Masculinity
For many years the Jewish community has held a unique definition of masculinity. While others favored brawn, we valued brains. Our

national and historical heroes are rabbis and learned men, statesmen, holy men and miracle workers. Jews never idolized men of physical power, aggression, warfare, or cruelty. Why?

There is a logical historical reason. For so long Jewish men were powerless vis-à-vis the general society, and there was no way to "compete" with the masculine norms of the non-Jewish world. Stripped of their right to bear arms in a violent society, deprived of voting rights until Emancipation, constrained in their choice of careers and professions, how were Jewish men, noncitizens, non-landed, non-gentry, to define themselves if not in opposition to the prevailing ideas of masculinity in their time? Aviva Cantor writes:

> On the one hand, there was the necessity for Jewish men to compensate for having been deprived of power vis-à-vis the men of the general society. Exile deprived them of the ability to engage in physical aggression and of using it to defend women and children and the community from attack. Exile reduced men to the powerlessness associated with women. . . . The rabbis ingeniously resolved this conflict by changing the concept of what constituted male power, and even more fundamentally (since power is part of the definition of manhood) what constituted masculinity. They stripped male power of the glorification and practice of violence, of rugged individualism, rapacious exploitation, machismo, rampant cruelty, conquest, military prowess, physical heroism, and the abuse of women. They redefined power as knowledge, learning and studying. They defined manhood itself in terms of commitment to and achievement in learning Torah. Thus they replaced the classic patriarchal definition of masculinity, of man-as-macho fighter, with the alternative definition of man-as-scholar.[1]

Man-as-scholar became the Jewish form of machismo, and so it essentially remains to this day. But this redefinition was not without its price. To retain some sense of elitism, to be sure the learning of Torah was utterly attractive as a central element of self-definition for men, it also served as a bonding experience for men. The yeshivahs thus became places where men would go to "retreat" from the world at large, and also from the world of women. The synagogue, not the battlefield, became the place where men could prove their mettle.

This was not possible if women were accorded the same privileges and opportunities there.

Today, many other definitions of masculinity are open to men. The synagogue is no longer a proving ground for masculinity. Because of that, it has also suffered. Many have noticed the "flight" of men from egalitarian synagogues as more and more women take leadership roles. What is this flight about? Is it about the last male bastion being stormed, or about the feeling of not being "needed" anymore, or about a male devaluation of something as soon as it becomes open to women, or about a genuine frustration with the "feminization" of today's Judaism? These are questions that must be answered by the men who take their Judaism seriously and who wish the next generation of boys to do so as well.

Judaism and Sexuality

The second area we must redefine is our definition of Jewish womanhood. Much of this definition rests on a heterosexual model and still depends upon marriage and motherhood as its locus. As a group, Jewish gays and lesbians seem welcome into our congregations when they act "like everyone else," that is, when they form monogamous relationships, join as families, have baby namings and *b'nei mitzvah.* But like the struggle years ago for women to be recognized as women, gays and lesbians are struggling to be recognized as such. Rebecca Alpert addresses that recognition on several fronts. She writes, "As sexual beings, we share the stigma that is attached to male homosexuality in Judaism, based on Biblical prohibitions. As feminists, we are part of the invisibility of women in Jewish tradition. As gender nonconformists, we defy the rigid approach to gender roles in traditional texts."[2] Jews who chafe at strict gender identifications and gender roles feel even more acutely the tradition's insistence on defining a Jew not only as a Jew, but specifically as a Jewish man (with his subsequent privileges and responsibilities as such) or a Jewish woman (with her subsequent privileges and responsibilities as such).

The Torah presents us with difficult texts on homosexuality. Male homosexual acts are called "abominations" in Leviticus 18:22. In Leviticus 20:13, stoning is the punishment for male homosexuality.

While there is no specific prohibition against lesbianism, that does not signal a permission for it. The absence of mention more likely stems from both a patriarchal inability to imagine a woman deriving sexual satisfaction without a man and a male-dominated biblical culture, more concerned with the emission of semen than in what women do with other women.

Some biblical commentators contend with the Leviticus passages by noting that these prohibitions hinge on an unclear word, *to-eivah,* which is generally translated as "abomination." Some suggest that homosexuality leads a man astray from his main duty of procreation, to abandon women (i.e., their wives) and to disrupt family life. Modern commentators have asked whether the Torah is concerned more with sexual acts than sexual relationships. The society of the Torah would not have known about loving homosexual relationships but rather about pagan homosexual relationships in which mostly older men used and possibly abused younger boys for their own sexual pleasure. This was not a loving relationship between equals, but rather a power imbalance using sex. Others fix upon the second half of the Levitical verse, "a man shall not lie with a man *as with a woman*," to question whether the text means homosexual sex should not be imitative of heterosexual sex. That is, a man should not lie with a man the way he would with a woman, nor should he ask his male partner to "play the part" of a woman. This would also suggest that in a patriarchal society, it would indeed be abhorrent for a man to *choose* to be "like a woman" when he is in the privileged class. Why would any man, no matter what his sexual orientation be, choose to act sexually like a woman, the passive, often "captured" partner? Or perhaps the text is warning heterosexual men not to attempt a "one-night" homosexual fling, using the man as he would a woman.

While the Torah says nothing about female homosexuality, the Rabbis of the Talmud, in *Y'vamot* 76a, were concerned with lesbianism only as a minor infraction, one they considered not a sin but "lewdness." Such women who "rub up against each other" were declared unfit to marry a *kohein.* Maimonides elaborates on this further in the *Mishneh Torah* by forbidding women to "engage in the doings of Egypt." Yet he assures the reader that a woman who engages in lesbianism is not prohibited to her husband (it is not considered adultery), but rather she should be flogged for "rebelliousness." Here again we see that lesbianism is considered a social act as much as a sexual one, one that threatens the patriarchal order. Such texts make it nearly impossible for Jews to discuss the visibility and full inclusion of gays and lesbians without the baggage of received tradition and years of hearing these biblical prohibitions read from the pulpit, seen as normative and acceptable.

Integration

Finally, we come to the question of identity altogether. What makes one a Jew? What makes one a woman? How is identity formed? Childhood influences and childhood memories form a large core of how we see ourselves. Our past relationships inform us over and over again. Societal pressures and mores exert a strong influence on us. We are not only created from birth, but we are also built from the world around us.

As adults, we re-create and rebuild ourselves. Sometimes we do so from scratch, and sometimes we piece ourselves together and weave an identity from all the various experiences we have had. Societal change impacts upon us, as well. Our values change as we form strong bonds. Change is a catalyst for identity reformation. In other words, none of us is the same as we were when we were children.

This is strongly felt by today's older women, who grew up in an era when change in the expectations and standards for women was rapid and nonstop. Younger women take for granted the "normalization" of women's new roles and rights. Sometimes the two generations are in conflict over this, and sometimes they can learn from each other's struggles or lack of struggle.

For some Jewish women, feminism is not an issue. There is an assumed equality or comfort with gender-based expectations. Those women may not identify as Jewish feminists, and yet all the changes brought about by feminism's impact on Judaism affect them, as well.

For other Jewish women, feminism "brought them back" to Judaism. For yet others, Judaism's ultimate sense of justice and equality brought them to feminism. Either way, there is no doubt that the Jewish world is immeasurably different now because of the presence, study, leadership, and vision of women. What that difference will look like in the future is up to each of us.

THE TEXTS

1. Aviva Cantor, *Jewish Women, Jewish Men: The Legacy of Patriarchy in Jewish Life* (San Francisco: Harper San Francisco, 1995), 99, 106:

   > When study and public performance of ritual—the components of spiritual resistance—came to be regarded as the most important endeavors in the Jewish struggle for survival, and the ones that defined masculinity, the role of the Jewish women as enabler became to facilitate those pursuits and to accept/endure exclusion from them.... Preventing women's intrusion upon this turf involved the classic Jewish behavioral methodology of channeling women's love of Torah into enabling.

2. Rebecca Alpert, *Like Bread on the Seder Plate: Jewish Lesbians and the Transformation of Tradition* (New York: Columbia University Press, 1997), 11:

   > Queer theory questions social constructions of dichotomies such as homo and heterosexual. Its goal is to eradicate fundamental social distinctions based on sex, gender, and sexual orientation and also to do away with the power relations that accrue according to these categories.

3. Barbara Breitman, "Jewish Masculinity in a New Light," in *A Mentsch among Men: Explorations in Jewish Masculinity,* ed. Harry Brod (Freedom, Calif.: The Crossings Press, 1988), 112:

   > Jewish men may well experience themselves, and be experienced by Jewish women as somehow less masculine than men of the dominant culture; Jewish women may well experience themselves, and be experienced by Jewish men as somehow less feminine than women of the dominant culture. Although Jewish women and men may blame each other for this phenomena, the insidious process has its roots in anti-Semitism.... In a patriarchal culture, which, paradoxically, has robbed its boys (and girls) of their natural fathers, tied men to unconscious dependence in women, cut men off from the love of other men, it is Jewish men who became the bearers of the Shadow, made to represent that Man other men were terrified of becoming. Through the mythology of anti-Semitism, Jewish men were cast as the "feminine man," the "cas-

trated man," the man dominated by a woman," "the man without a land," in a world of warring nations, warring men.

4. Jeffrey Salkin, *Searching for My Brothers: Jewish Men in a Gentile World* (New York: G. P. Putnam's Sons, 1999), 218–19:

> The image of God as Father can actually teach men about fatherhood. . . . Just as there is God-hunger in many of us, there is father-hunger as well. . . . The fatherly aspect of God is one of firmness and fairness, active when necessary and compassionate when desirable. It means the creative combination of both distance and intimacy, of the urge to love and the need to control.

THE QUESTIONS

1. Can we speak of a male Jewish feminism? What would it look like if men were passionate and involved in what we now call "women's issues"? Why do you think such areas as violence against women, child care, health care, child poverty, literacy, and others have become seen as "women's issues"? How can we make them into "Jewish issues"?

2. How would you feel if men in your congregation began to form "men's spirituality" groups, went on male-only retreats to study men and Judaism, or hosted a weekend of seminars and speakers on men and male roles in the Bible for a men's special Shabbat?

3. Comment on Aviva Cantor's theory that study of Torah became closed to women to guard it as a safe haven for men to define their masculinity.

4. Comment on Rebecca Alpert's quote that homosexual or hetero-sexual is a dichotomy created by social construct and the idea that, in fact, all sexual identity and all definitions of masculinity and femininity are socially ordained. Do you think there are any dif-ferences between men and women that are innate or biological? Can you imagine a society in which masculinity and femininity were not defined?

5. Many single Jews who try dating within the Jewish community complain that Jewish men and Jewish women simply don't like each other. Jewish men seem unappealing; Jewish women over-powering. Comment on this in light of Breitman's quote. Do you think there is some truth to these stereotypes? Do you think these stereotypes play any part in interdating and intermarriage? How can we heal the rift between Jewish men and women?

6. Do you agree with Salkin that an image of God as father can be helpful for human fathers? Why or why not? Does seeing God in this light make male God language less of a problem? Do you agree that "the creative combination of both distance and intimacy,

of the urge to love and the need to control" is a male characteristic?

7. What do you think the next pressing issues for Jewish women will be?

Notes

Chapter 1. Feminist Analysis and Torah Study

1. Elyse Goldstein, *ReVisions: Seeing Torah through a Feminist Lens* (Woodstock, Vt.: 1998), 70.

Chapter 2. "Womanhood" in the Tanach: Persons or Property?

1. Paula Cooey, quoted in Elyse Goldstein, *ReVisions: Seeing Torah through a Feminist Lens* (Woodstock, Vt.: 1998), 70.

Chapter 3. Eishet Chayil: "A Woman of Valor" as Paradigm

1. Carol A. Newsome and Sharon H. Ringe, eds., *The Women's Bible Commentary* (Louisville, Ky.: Westminster/John Knox Press, 1992), 151.
2. See, for example, Genesis 47:6, Exodus 18:21, and Deuteronomy 3:18.

Chapter 4. Time-Bound Mitzvot

1. Judith Plaskow, "The Right Question is Theological," in *On Being a Jewish Feminist: A Reader,* ed. Susannah Heschel (New York: Schocken Books, 1983), 224.
2. Carole Gilligan, *In a Different Voice* (Cambridge, Mass.: Harvard University Press, 1993).
3. Rachel Biale, *Women and Jewish Law* (New York: Schocken Books, 1984), 10–12.

Chapter 5. Blood and Water: The Menstrual and Mikveh Laws

1. Mary Douglas, *Purity and Danger* (London: Routledge and Kegan Paul, 1996), 120.

2. Aryeh Kaplan, *Waters of Eden: The Mystery of the Mikveh* (New York: NCSY/Union of Orthodox Jewish Congregations, 1976), 14.

Chapter 6. Rosh Chodesh

1. *Pirkei D'Rabbi Eliezer* 45; see also Babylonian Talmud, *M'gillah* 22b. For more information on the history and modern interpretations of Rosh Chodesh and its celebrations, see Susan Berrin, ed., *Celebrating the New Moon: A Rosh Chodesh Anthology* (Northvale, N.J.: Jason Aronson, 1996).
2. Joseph H. Hertz, ed., *Authorized Daily Prayerbook* (New York: Bloch Publishing Company, 1957), 995.
3. Robin Zeigler, "My Body, My Self and Rosh Chodesh," in *Celebrating the New Moon: A Rosh Chodesh Anthology,* ed. Susan Berrin (Northvale, N.J.: Jason Aronson, 1996), 38.

Chapter 9. Women and the Synagogue

1. See Bernadette Brooten, *Women as Leaders in the Ancient Synagogue* (Atlanta: Scholars Press, 1982).

Chapter 10. God Language and Theological Issues

1. Judith Plaskow, *Standing Again at Sinai* (San Francisco: Harper San Francisco, 1990), 123.

Chapter 11. The Shechinah

1. Lynn Gottlieb, *She Who Dwells Within: A Feminist Vision of a Renewed Judaism* (New York: Harper San Francisco, 1995) 7.
2. Ibid., 7–9
3. *Kuzari* 2:20, 23; 3:23. For a more complete discussion of the *Shechinah* in Jewish tradition, see *Encyclopedia Judaica,* vol. 14, s.v. "Shechinah."

Chapter 12. The Question of Changing Liturgy

1. See Marcia Falk, *Book of Blessings* (San Francisco: HarperCollins, 1996).

Chapter 14. Where Do We Go from Here? Men, Sexuality, and Integration

1. Aviva Cantor, *Jewish Women, Jewish Men: The Legacy of Patriarchy in Jewish Life* (San Francisco: Harper San Francisco, 1995), 92–93.
2. Rebecca Alpert, *Like Bread on the Seder Plate: Jewish Lesbians and the Transformation of Tradition* (New York: Columbia University Press, 1997), 8.

Bibliography

Torah Commentaries, General

Englemayer, Shammai, Joseph S. Ozarowski, and David M. Sofian. *Common Ground: The Weekly Torah Portion through the Eyes of a Conservative, Orthodox, and Reform Rabbi.* Northvale, N.J.: Jason Aronson, 1998.

Fields, Harvey J. *A Torah Commentary for Our Times.* New York: UAHC Press, 1998.

Fox, Everett, ed. *The Five Books of Moses: Genesis, Exodus, Leviticus, Numbers, Deuteronomy: A New Translation with Introductions, Commentary, and Notes.* New York: Schocken Books, 1995.

Grishaver, Joel Lurie. *Learning Torah: A Self-Guided Journey through the Layers of Jewish Learning.* New York: UAHC Press, 1998.

Kushner, Lawrence S., and Kerry M. Olitzky. *Sparks Beneath the Surface: A Spiritual Commentary on the Torah.* Northvale, N.J.: Jason Aronson, 1995.

Leibowitz, Nehama. *Studies in Bereshit, Shmot, Vayikra, Bamidbar, Devarim.* Jerusalem: World Zionist Organization, 1980.

Moyers, Bill D. *Genesis: A Living Conversation* (PBS Series). New York: Doubleday, 1997.

Peli, Pinchas. *Torah Today: A Renewed Encounter with Scripture.* Washington D.C.: B'nai Brith Books, 1987.

Plaut, Gunther, ed. *The Torah: A Modern Commentary.* New York: UAHC Press, 1981; 12th rev. ed., 1998.

Sarna, Nahum M. *Understanding Genesis.* New York: Schocken Books, 1970.

———. *Exploring Exodus.* New York: Schocken Books, 1987.

———, general ed. *The JPS Torah Commentary.* Philadelphia: Jewish Publication Society, 1991.

Feminist Biblical Interpretation

Adler, Rachel. "In Your Blood, Live: Re-Visions of a Theology of Purity." *Tikkun Magazine* 8, no.1 (Jan./Feb. 1993).

Antonelli, Judith S. *In the Image of God: A Feminist Commentary on the Torah.* Northvale, N.J.: Jason Aronson, 1997.

Bellis, Alice Ogden. *Helpmates, Harlots, and Heroes: Women's Stories in the Hebrew Bible.* Louisville, Ky.: Westminster John Knox Press, 1994.

Bird, Phyllis A. *Missing Persons and Mistaken Identities: Women and Gender in Ancient Israel.* Philadelphia: Fortress Press, 1997.

Brenner, Athalya, ed. *Feminist Companion to Reading the Bible: Approaches, Methods, and Strategies.* Ithaca, N.Y.: Cornell University Press, 1997.

Buchmann, Christina, and Celina Spiegel, eds. *Out of the Garden: Women Writers on the Bible.* New York: Fawcett Columbine, 1994.

Exum, J. Cheryl. *Fragmented Women: Feminist Subversions of Biblical Narratives.* Harrisburg, Pa.: Trinity Press International, 1993.

Feigenson, Emily, ed. *Beginning the Journey.* New York: Women of Reform Judaism, 1997.

Frankel, Ellen. *The Five Books of Miriam.* New York: G. P. Putnam's Sons, 1996.

Goldstein, Elyse. *ReVisions: Seeing Torah through a Feminist Lens.* Woodstock, Vt.: Jewish Lights, 1998.

———, ed. *The Women's Torah Commentary.* Woodstock, Vt.: Jewish Lights, 2000.

Meyers, Carol. *Discovering Eve: Ancient Israelite Women in Context.* New York: Oxford University Press, 1991.

Newsom, Carol A., and Sharon H. Ringe, eds. *The Women's Bible Commentary.* Louisville, Ky.: Westminster John Knox Press, 1992.

Orenstein, Debra, and Jane Rachel Litman, eds. *Lifecycles,* vol. 2, *Jewish Women on Biblical Themes in Contemporary Life.* Woodstock, Vt.: Jewish Lights, 1997.

Pardes, Ilana. *Countertraditions in the Bible.* Cambridge, Mass.: Harvard University Press, 1992.

Schussler Fiorenza, Elisabeth. *Bread Not Stone: The Challenge of Feminist Biblical Interpretation.* Boston: Beacon Press, 1995.

Tolbert, Mary Ann. "Defining the Problem: The Bible and Feminist Hermeneutics," *Semeia* 28 (1983).

Trible, Phyllis. *Texts of Terror: Literary-Feminist Readings of Biblical Narratives.* Philadelphia: Fortress Press, 1984.

Female Biblical Characters

Bach, Alice, ed. *Women in the Hebrew Bible: A Reader.* New York: Routledge Press, 1998.

Bronner, Leila Leah. *From Eve to Esther.* Louisville, Ky.: Westminster John Knox Press, 1994.

Burns, Rita J. *Has the Lord Indeed Spoken Only through Moses?* Dissertation Series. Atlanta: Scholars Press, 1987.

Dame, Enid, Lilly Rivlin, Henny Wenkart, and Naomi Wolf, eds. *Which Lilith?: Feminist Writers Re-Create the World's First Woman.* Northvale, N.J.: Jason Aronson, 1998.

Diamant, Anita. *The Red Tent.* New York: St. Martin's Press, 1997.

Handelman, Susan, and Ora Wiskind-Elper, eds. *Torah of the Mothers.* Israel: Urim Publications, 2000.

Hyman, Naomi Mara. *Biblical Women in the Midrash: A Sourcebook.* Northvale, N.J.: Jason Aronson, 1998.

Jeansonne, Sharon Pace. *The Women of Genesis.* Minneapolis: Fortress Press, 1990.

Koltuv, Barbara Black. *The Book of Lilith.* York Beach, Me.: Nicolas-Hays, 1987.

Labowitz, Shoni. *God, Sex, and Women of the Bible: Discovering Our Sensual, Spiritual Selves.* New York: Simon & Schuster, 1998.

Phillips, J. A. *Eve: The History of an Idea.* San Francisco: Harper and Row, 1984.

Rosen, Norma. *Biblical Women Unbound.* Philadelphia: Jewish Publication Society, 1996.

Teubal, Savina J. *Ancient Sisterhood: The Lost Traditions of Hagar and Sarah.* Columbus: Ohio University Press, 1997.

Thaw Ronson, Barbara L. *The Women of the Torah: Commentaries from the Talmud, Midrash, and Kabbalah.* Northvale, N.J.: Jason Aronson, 1998.

Zones, Jane Sprague, ed. *Taking the Fruit: Modern Women's Tales of the Bible.* Chico, Calif.: Women's Institute for Continuing Jewish Education, 1981.

Women and Halachah

Berkovitz, Eliezer. *Jewish Women in Time and Torah.* Hoboken, N.J.: Ktav, 1990.

Berrin, Susan, ed. *Celebrating the New Moon: A Rosh Chodesh Anthology.* Northvale, N.J.: Jason Aronson, 1996.

Biale, Rachel. *Women and Jewish Law.* New York: Schocken Books, 1984.

Hauptman, Judith. *Rereading the Rabbis: A Woman's Voice.* Boulder, Colo.: Westview Press, 1999.

Wasserfall, Rahel R. *Women and Water: Menstruation in Jewish Life and Law.* Waltham, Mass.: Brandeis University Press, 1999.

Women as Rabbis

Berman, Donna, ed. "Wisdom You Are My Sister: 25 Years of Women in the Rabbinate." *CCAR Journal: A Reform Jewish Quarterly* 44 (summer 1997).

Greenberg, Simon, ed. *The Ordination of Women as Rabbis: Studies and Responsa.* Moreshet Series: Studies in Jewish History, Literature, and Thought, vol. 14. New York: Jewish Theological Seminary, 1988.

Nadell, Pamela Susan. *Women Who Would Be Rabbis: A History of Women's Ordination, 1889–1985.* Boston: Beacon Press, 1998.

Zola, Gary Phillip, ed. *Women Rabbis: Exploration and Celebration: Papers Delivered at an Academic Conference Honoring Twenty Years of Women in the Rabbinate, 1972–1992.* Cinncinnati: Hebrew Union College Press, 1996.

On Gender, Masculinity, and Sexuality

Alpert, Rebecca. *Like Bread on the Seder Plate: Jewish Lesbians and the Transformation of Tradition*. New York: Columbia University Press, 1997.

Balka, Christie, and Andy Rose, eds. *Twice Blessed: On Being Lesbian or Gay and Jewish*. Boston: Beacon Press, 1989.

Beck, Evelyn Torten, ed. *Nice Jewish Girls: A Lesbian Anthology*. Boston: Beacon Press, 1989.

Boyarin, Daniel. *Unheroic Conduct: The Rise of Heterosexuality and the Invention of the Jewish Man*. Berkeley, Calif.: University of California Press, 1997.

Brod, Harry, ed. *A Mentsch among Men: Explorations in Jewish Masculinity*. Freedom, Calif.: The Crossings Press, 1988.

Cantor, Aviva. *Jewish Women, Jewish Men: The Legacy of Patriarchy in Jewish Life*. San Francisco: Harper San Francisco, 1995.

Grishaver, Joel Lurie. *The Bonding of Isaac: Stories and Essays about Gender and Jewish*. Los Angeles: Alef Design Group, 1996.

Salkin, Jeffrey. *Searching for My Brothers: Jewish Men in a Gentile World*. New York: G. P. Putnam's Sons, 1999.

Women, Feminism, and Judaism

Adler, Rachel. *Engendering Judaism: An Inclusive Theology and Ethics*. Philadelphia: Jewish Publication Society, 1998.

Brooten, Bernadette. *Women as Leaders in the Ancient Synagogue*. Atlanta: Scholars Press, 1982.

Davidman, Lynn, and Shelly Tenenbaum, eds. *Feminist Perspectives on Jewish Studies*. New Haven: Yale University Press, 1994.

Frankiel, Tamar. *The Voice of Sarah: Feminine Spirituality and Traditional Judaism*. San Francisco: Harper and Row, 1990.

Gill-Jaffe, Ellen, ed. *The Jewish Woman's Book of Wisdom: Thoughts from Prominent Jewish Women on Spirituality, Identity, Sisterhood, Family, and Faith*. New York: Birch Lane Press, 1998.

Greenberg, Blu. *On Women and Judaism: A View from Tradition*. Philadelphia: Jewish Publication Society, 1981.

Grossman, Susan, and Rivka Haut, eds. *Daughters of the King: Women and the Synagogue*. Philadephia: Jewish Publication Society, 1992.

Heschel, Susannah, ed. *On Being a Jewish Feminist*. New York: Schocken Books, 1995.

Orenstein, Debra. *Lifecycles,* vol. 1, *Jewish Women on Life Passages and Personal Milestones*. Woodstock, Vt.: Jewish Lights, 1994.

Peskowitz, Miriam, and Laura Levitt, eds. *Judaism Since Gender*. New York: Routledge, 1997.

Plaskow, Judith. *Standing Again at Sinai*. San Francisco: Harper San Francisco, 1990.

Plaskow, Judith, and Carole Christ. *Weaving the Visions: New Patterns in Feminist Spirituality*. San Francisco: HarperCollins, 1989.

Rothschild, Sylvia, and Sybil Sheridan, eds. *Taking Up the Timbrel*. London: SCM Press, 2000.

Schneider, Susan Weidman. *Jewish and Female: A Guide and Sourcebook for Today's Jewish Woman*. New York: Simon and Schuster, 1985.

Umansky, Ellen, and Diane Ashton, eds. *Four Centuries of Jewish Women's Spirituality: A Sourcebook*. Boston: Beacon Press, 1992.

Zolty, Shoshana Pantel. *"And All Your Children Shall Be Learned": Women and the Study of Torah in Jewish Law and History*. Northvale, N.J.: Jason Aronson, 1997.

On God and God Language

Campbell, Joseph, and Charles Muses, eds. *In All Her Names*. San Francisco: Harper San Francisco, 1991.

Falk, Marcia. *The Book of Blessings*. San Francisco: HarperCollins, 1996.

Frymer-Kensky, Tikva. *In the Wake of the Goddess*. New York: MacMillan, 1992.

Goldenberg, Naomi R. *Changing of the Gods*. Boston: Beacon Press, 1979.

Gottlieb, Lynn. *She Who Dwells Within: A Feminist Vision of a Renewed Judaism*. San Francisco: Harper San Francisco, 1995.

Graves, Robert. *The White Goddess*. London: Faber and Faber, 1961.

Graves, Robert, and Raphael Patai. *Hebrew Myths*. Garden City, N.Y.: Doubleday and Co., 1964.

Patai, Raphael. *The Hebrew Goddess*. Detroit: Wayne State University Press, 1990.

Plaskow, Judith. "Facing the Ambiguity of God." *Tikkun Magazine* 6, no. 5 (September/October 1991).

Roundtable Discussion. "If God Is God She Is Not Nice." *Journal of Feminist Studies in Religion* 5, no. 1 (spring 1989).

Stone, Merlin. *When God Was a Woman*. New York: Dial Press, 1976.

Weaver, Mary Jo. "Who Is the Goddess and Where Does She Get Us?" and "Can a Sexist Model Liberate Us? Ancient Near Eastern 'Fertility' Goddesses." *Journal of Feminist Studies in Religion* 5, no. 1 (spring 1989).